**FINDING A JOB**

# Win the Job at the Interview

*Sarah Berry*

WARD LOCK

**A WARD LOCK BOOK**

First published in the UK 1997

by Ward Lock

Wellington House
125 Strand
LONDON
WC2R 0BB

A Cassell Imprint

Copyright © Sarah Berry 1997

All rights reserved. No part of this publication may be reproduced in any material form (including photocopying or storing it in any medium by electronic means and whether or not transiently or incidentally to some other use of this publication) without the written permission of the copyright owner, except in accordance with the provisions of the Copyright, Designs and Patents Act 1988 or under the terms of a licence issued by the Copyright Licensing Agency, 90 Tottenham Court Road, London W1P 9HE. Applications for the copyright owner's written permission to reproduce any part of this publication should be addressed to the publisher.

Distributed in the United States

by Sterling Publishing Co., Inc.

387 Park Avenue South, New York, NY 10016-8810

A British Library Cataloguing in Publication Data block for this book may be obtained from the British Library.

ISBN   0 7063 7611 0

Designed and typeset by Ben Cracknell Studios

Printed and bound in Great Britain by
Creative Print and Design Wales, Ebbw Vale.

# Contents

1 *Introduction* 7
2 *Overcoming Interview Fears* 21
3 *Being Prepared* 35
4 *Asking Constructive Questions* 61
5 *Dos and Don'ts* 69
6 *Closing the Interview* 76
7 *Alternative Interviews* 79
8 *Assessing the Offer* 88
9 *Conclusion* 98
  *Appendix – Useful Forms* 101
  *Index* 107

# ONE

# Introduction

Confident job candidates perform well at interviews. They project a good image of themselves and their abilities and they make it their business to do their homework beforehand. They research the company and gain interview practice. In short, they sell themselves, but more importantly they *inspire* the employer's confidence. Thus, confident interviewees are the successful ones. For they give the employer more reason to say 'yes' to choosing them than to say 'no'. Hence it is in your interest to develop the same degree of self-confidence. This book will show you how to do this. The good news is that it is not as difficult as you might think!

## Confidence

Self-confidence is rooted in experience, knowledge and practice. If you lack confidence or have had yours knocked by circumstances, don't despair because, given time and patience, it can be rebuilt. This book lays down the types of qualities that you need to develop in order to give a good interview performance. Qualities such as:

- Talking succinctly about yourself.
- Expressing verbally your key qualities and skills in a saleable way.
- Being comfortable with the interview format.

- ✔ Presenting ideas and concepts in front of an audience/interview panel.
- ✔ Being brave enough to listen to yourself on tape, or watch yourself on video camera and to recognize and correct slight flaws in your delivery.
- ✔ Expressing your key needs and requirements at the interview.
- ✔ Remaining open-minded and honest throughout the interview to ensure that you meet your needs.
- ✔ Interacting on a one-to-one basis or as part of a small group.
- ✔ Thinking on your feet and expressing yourself in a businesslike way.
- ✔ Learning from your mistakes and using it to win the ultimate prize – the job offer.

If you can develop and perfect some or even all of the above qualities, you will set yourself apart from the less confident candidates.

## INSPIRING CONFIDENCE

Inspiring confidence in others is not easy to do, and it is harder still if you are a bit nervous. The key, however, is to not let the nerves take over so that you become so knotted up that your words don't come out properly and your body's movements are either shaky or fixed rigid.

It is natural to be slightly nervous and the increase in adrenalin should help you to be more alert and to think more clearly. Chapter 2 suggests ways to deal with any interview fears so that interviewees can direct their attention away from their nervousness towards the aim of inspiring the employer's confidence in them.

The way to inspire confidence at an interview is to confirm and reconfirm throughout the interview the following three points:

- that you have the ability to do the job.

- that you want the job.
- that you will fit in with the organization – its style, management and philosophies.

If you can, through your answers, address the employer's concerns about you, then you give him/her the required assurances in your abilities.

Although it may seem unnatural to answer the questions in this way, it is necessary to do this in order to address the employer's concerns about you. For the employer has fears too, such as the fear that you won't turn out to be as good as you make yourself out to be. So your answers need to convince him that you really are the best and right person for the job on offer. Otherwise the employer will lose interest in you and find reasons to reject you. If you want feedback on your performance, be bold and ask him/her, before the end of the interview, 'Have I convinced you that I am capable and worthy of this job?' If you haven't convinced the employer, he/she will normally say, 'I am concerned about this or that'. Then you have another chance to put the record straight. A question of this kind works well and demonstrates your self-confidence at its height. You are not afraid of the answer, whatever it may be!

## Interviews

The purpose of an interview is:

- to meet you face-to-face.
- to learn more about you, your ideas and your way of thinking.
- to talk about your skills and strengths.
- to assess your personality.
- to discover your potential.
- to see how you interact with others.

- to discuss your aspirations and ambitions.
- for you to assess whether this is the job for you; whether or not it fulfils your short- and long-term career plans.

Thus, interviews are a two-way process of discovery – for you to learn about the job and for the employer to get to know you. It is *as* crucial for you to choose the job as it is for the employer to choose you.

## WHAT ARE YOUR CHANCES OF SECURING THE JOB?

Most interviewees weigh up their chances of success beforehand. No one enjoys being rejected, but you will perform better if you resist the temptation to think that you need the job, you deserve the job or even that the job is all but yours. Nothing in life is guaranteed and anything could go wrong or change. Anyway, you don't want to increase the pressure. The fact of the matter is that you stand as good a chance as any of the other interviewees of being offered the job.

Employers don't waste time seeing unsuitable candidates. On paper, you probably match the employer's desired criteria, such as the necessary qualifications, work experience, level of responsibility and training gained. So keep a level head and remain calm at all times, for there is no such thing as almost having a job; it is either one thing or the other. Do your preparation beforehand and work hard in the actual interview and *then* the showing off is all yours.

## THE INTERVIEW ITSELF

The key is to relax. No one is going to trick or embarrass you. In fact you have everything to gain because the interviewer wants, indeed has chosen, to see you. Arrive in good time, leaving a few minutes to smarten and freshen yourself up, but go easy on the aftershave and perfume. Check in as instructed, and leave any luggage at the reception or in the waiting room. Steady your nerves by reading the paper or company brochures rather than just sitting doing nothing. Remember it is too late to rehearse now, but you will be fine.

When called, don't rush or be rushed. Take your time and walk calmly, as it is not unheard of for an interviewee to fall or trip into the room! To help calm the nerves, take a deep breath, walk in and, most importantly, greet the interviewer(s) with a firm handshake and a friendly smile.

## STRUCTURE OF AN INTERVIEW

The interview itself will usually last between half an hour and an hour. It is normal to be interviewed by one or two people and in certain circumstances you could have a panel of interviewers. If this is the case, normally only one person asks the majority of questions and the others will only ask questions at the end, when they are invited to do so. The panel members are there to listen to your answers and take notes, not to disapprove of you. So, to avoid being intimidated, focus your attention on the person asking the questions and occasionally involve the others by glancing at them when appropriate.

During the interview, it is usual to be seated at a desk or table opposite the interviewer or in easy chairs facing each other. There are certain circumstances where you could feel that you are faced with a power battle because your chair is considerably lower than the others or it is placed in the middle of a room or in direct sunlight. However, although it is possible that your chair has been deliberately put in an inferior position, it is far more likely that a genuine error has been made. Judge each situation as it arises, and follow your instincts. If you feel uncomfortable say something, but casually rather than aggressively. Ask if it would be all right to sit in another chair.

On the whole, most interviewers play it straight. They are busy people and have far more to do with their time than play power games with interviewees.

## THE FORMAT OF INTERVIEWS

An interview is a designated period of time when you and the interviewer have a civilized conversation in order to learn more about each other. You greet each other, and then engage in a bit of idle chitchat. The interviewer will follow this by asking you some questions. After that, the interviewer will give you an opportunity to ask your questions. These will be answered and then you will formally say goodbye and leave.

In principle, this is an easy process. However, while all this is taking place, the interviewer will pay attention not only to what you say but also to how you respond. The interviewer will evaluate your answers and reactions. On the basis of this he/she will come to an informed decision about your ability to do the job, your qualifications, your reliability, adaptability, and whether your personality will fit in with the company, the department and current employees. In short, everything will be scrutinized.

Thus, to enable you to give a smooth and convincing performance, think about the types of topics that are likely to crop up. Also, spend some time thinking about how you would respond. Above all, practise your answers out loud, and where possible video yourself or tape your answers. Play it back and look and listen hard. Is this the real you or do you need to work on your tone, pitch or inflection?

### Questions

Interviews are all about questions – questions that probe, questions that put you on the spot and questions that you might prefer not to answer! However, the key is to take your time, remain calm and be up front. The questions asked and the answers you give will make up the majority of the conversation at the interview. Questions are asked for a specific purpose, but they also give you an indication and an insight into the company itself. For example, you may learn about the philosophies of the company; the level of commitment required by employees; the emphasis on career or succession planning; the motivation of the employees; and the style of management. Above all, you will find out about the culture of the organization. These are all things that will help you to decide whether this is the kind of company you wish to work for. It is always best to give honest and brief answers.

Sometimes an interviewee can feel that the interviewer is trying to antagonize or draw him/her into an argument. If so, either ignore it, or confront the issue. You could say that you get the impression from the question that the interviewer wants to hear your opinion – is this right? Then you will put the interviewer on the spot and get a fair answer. The interviewer will either back off or adopt a less threatening approach. In many jobs to have an opinion is important and a vital asset. The company may want employees to be able to stand up for themselves, the team and the product, rather than having an individual that is either bullied or steamrollered in action. So, if invited to do so, give your opinion.

It is usual for most interviewers to want to control the discussions in order to cover certain areas. In fact some organizations go so far as to ask each candidate the same question, so that a comparison can be made of all the responses. Interviewers control the discussions in a number of ways, as follows.

- **By setting the scene**. They may set the scene by indicating the role that is expected of the interviewee. This has the advantage of settling the interviewee's nerves, but it clearly indicates that the interviewer is in charge. Only inexperienced interviewers tend to allow the balance of power to be swung in favour of the interviewee, who can end up managing and directing the format of the interview. Lack of experience is normally the cause of this, rather than lack of character. Often companies overcome this hurdle by having a more experienced interviewer in the room who is there to redirect the conversation and questions when necessary. So, the interviewer may set the scene by stating, 'I will start by telling you a bit about the company, its profile and the job on offer, then I will ask you some questions, and then I will be pleased to answer any questions that you may want to raise about the job or company, at the end.'

- **By adopting moving-on techniques**. Another way to control and manage the interview is for the interviewer to refer to checklists. 'I wish to cover your background, education and present and past roles.' They may interrupt your answers by saying, 'Thank you, you have given enough information, now I would like to move on to…subject on my list.' Or they may ask you to answer a question 'briefly' or they just clock-watch throughout the interview to ensure that brief and succinct replies are given.

- **By using different styles of questioning**. This is the most powerful way to control the interview. It affects the way you reply, the information you give and also the judgements that are made about you. Awareness of the questioning styles can help interviewees vary responses and attitude to questions. Thus, it can stop interviewees taking offence when asked certain types of questions.

Questions affect the style of the interview and some may be easier than others to answer. It is unlikely that the questions will all be of the same type, but it can happen. If it does, it is a reflection of an inexperienced interviewer and not a reflection of you. The types of questions common to all interviews are listed below.

## OPEN QUESTIONS

These are questions to which it is impossible to give a 'yes' or 'no' answer. People will often not only reply with the fact and issues but also with their feelings and attitudes. Thus, the interviewer can form a picture about the person sitting in front of him/her and can either explore certain topics further or ask them to expand on their feelings. The only disadvantage about these questions is that you could say too much or you could start to dominate the interview. Examples of open questions are given opposite.

| | |
|---|---|
| **What** | What are your duties? |
| | What have you learnt from the situation? |
| | What type of management brings out the best in you? |
| **Why** | Why was that a problem for you? |
| | Why did that irritate you? |
| | Why did you decide to do ...? |
| **When** | When did that happen? |
| | When do you get bored? |
| **Where** | Where do you expect your next move to be? |
| | Where was that? |
| **Which** | Which part of the job did you most enjoy? |
| | Which part of the job did you dislike? |
| | Which areas of this job interest you? |
| **How** | How do you feel about ...? |
| | How did you get around that ? |
| | How did you get the job? |

Similar questions might start with openings such as:

- Please explain why that was important to you.
- In what way did you benefit from your training?

Some useful open-ended questions are given below.

- What prompted this decision?
- What kind of advice did you take?
- Why did you leave such and such a job?
- How do you intend to achieve ...?
- Have you any questions you would like to ask me?
- How much notice do you have to give your current employer?
- What activities are you involved in just now?

- How would you respond if you were offered the job?
- Looking back, what would you have done differently?
- What do you think the reason was for your dismissal?

## CLOSED QUESTIONS

At the other extreme are closed questions, which usually only produce a 'yes' or a 'no' answer. These are useful for checking pure facts and eliciting a direct response. They can also be used to stop the interviewee doing all the talking, or they are used to limit the less relevant parts of the interview. Examples of closed questions are given below.

- I see you worked for ...?
- I see you have ....
- Do you like ...?
- Do you have good health?
- Do you get on with ...?

Expect a few closed questions during the interview. However, if they become the norm you need to change the way you reply. Offer more than the straight 'yes' or 'no answer, perhaps by adding a bit more as well as giving the interviewer what he/she wants. Try to communicate as many positive and relevant facts about yourself as you can.

## PROBING QUESTIONS

Probing questions are the interviewer's most sophisticated and useful tool. They are used to clarify, to justify or to reveal strengths or weaknesses – areas that the interviewee may wish to hide. The questions tend to be quite specific and predictable, and they are normally used when the interviewee is being over-talkative or when the conversation is drifting a bit. Examples of probing questions are given below.

- What is your reason for saying that?
- Why does that concern you?
- Who else affected your decision?
- How did you resolve the situation?
- How did you react to ...?

## HYPOTHETICAL QUESTIONS

Interviewers often ask the 'What if?' question. It may be because this is an actual situation which you will have to face in the job, or it could be asked just to test your ability to think on your feet. Answer the question as best as you can and be able to back up your answer. Examples of hypothetical questions are given below.

- What would you do if you were short-staffed?
- What would you do if you had to deal with an angry customer?
- What would you do if two important people demanded your attention at the same time?

## LEADING QUESTIONS

On the whole these questions suggest the answer to give. Interviewers may wish you to disagree with the suggestion in order to hear your point of view, or the interviewer may be advising you of the company's rules and expectations. You can either agree or disagree depending upon how truthful it is. The choice is yours.

However, try to put your point across logically but not emotionally. These questions may help you to make your final choice about the company. Examples of leading questions are given below.

- The company has this philosophy; do you hold this philosophy?
- I wouldn't want to do ....; what about you?
- I suppose you got on with your previous boss?

## COMPLICATED QUESTIONS

These questions take two forms: the alternative question and the multiple question. The alternative question is in fact a closed question, but has two conflicting parts. For example:

- What part-time jobs did you have or didn't you bother because of your studies?

The tip with these questions is to ignore the bit that doesn't apply and respond only to the bit that does apply. The multiple question leads to confusion and vagueness because the interviewee doesn't know where to begin his answer. For example:

- Did you pick up new skills in your last post and what did you think of the facilities?

It is best that your reply acknowledges the two parts perhaps by saying something along the lines of: 'I will answer...first and then...bit second.'

## SUMMARIZING QUESTIONS

These are used by the interviewer to clarify and confirm what you have said.

- So what you are saying is....
- I understand that what you have said is .....

These are often used in technical professions, but remember the summarizing question is a tool that you too can use if you feel that a question needs further clarification.

## REFLECTING WHAT HAS BEEN SAID

The interviewer may reflect back what has been said in order to encourage less confident or more reticent interviewees to expand further. For example:

- So, you learnt a lot from that role?
- I expect that you did find it quite stressful.

This technique is used to show that the interviewer is listening but not making judgements on what has been said.

Whichever question style is used, try to communicate as much positive information as you can. Paranoia doesn't help your case, so avoid reading too much into a question. Try instead reflecting back on what you think has been asked, for greater clarity. Never be afraid to ask for the question to be rephrased or repeated. If you are not up to date or don't have in-depth knowledge on a subject, never bluff your way through the answer hoping for the best. Probing questions will be asked and that could be embarrassing for you.

Above all, talk fluently, and remember no one but you can put your case forward. It shouldn't be that difficult as long as you do the preparation. Preparation is dealt with in Chapter 3, and includes the types of topics and questions likely to crop up at interviews (see pages 45–59).

## THIS BOOK WILL DEMONSTRATE

**① How to build your confidence.**
To enable you to 'be yourself' at the interview, so that you can present the best and most saleable side of your personality.

**② How to recognize and respond to the different questioning tactics.**

**③ How to prepare question topics in advance.**
This will enable you to answer those difficult questions with ease.

**④ How to improve your personal grooming.**
It is essential that you are happy with your image, comfortable with how you look and in line with the company's image.

**⑤ How to assess the offer.**
Learn how to determine whether it is what you want and how solid an offer it really is.

**⑥ How to prepare a 'presentation' for the interview.**
Never be afraid of standing up in front of people again. Here you will learn what to cover, what to exclude, and what to have on standby in case of extra time.

**⑦ How to overcome typical interview nerves.**
Learn how to establish a rapport with the interviewer rather than regarding him or her as the enemy.

So, at interviews you need to be a more confident, well-groomed and assertive version of yourself – the kind of person employers are looking to employ.

# TWO

## *Overcoming Interview Fears*

Most people fear attending interviews. For beginners and people who have had bad experiences in the past, it can be especially nerve-racking. It seems to get even more daunting. It is not that they don't want the job, because they do, it is just that the process to achieve it is such a big hurdle. The actual thought of attending the interview creates panic. Negative thoughts take over, for example:

- will I get the job?
- will I be good enough?
- will I be able to answer all the questions?

It is normal to be nervous, and it often works to your advantage because you are sharper. However, it is necessary to strike a balance between being nervous and being gripped by panic. This chapter demonstrates how to calm the nerves and how to prepare, so that you can attend an interview with confidence and conviction.

Never forget that interviewers are looking for someone to fill their vacancy. Being selected for an interview means that you stand as good a chance as anyone of being chosen. In fact, interviewers want to choose someone from their shortlist, and that someone could be you. Interviewers are there to draw out the best from candidates; they are not there to trick, embarrass or ridicule them.

So remember that interviewers want the best from candidates and you want to be the best. An interview is a performance. It is your chance to shine through and sell your special qualities and skills. So prepare beforehand and it shouldn't be such an ordeal after all; it might perhaps even turn out to be an enjoyable experience.

## Are you afraid of the interview or the job?

Before looking at how to steady interview nerves, consider first whether you are nervous about the interview or about the job itself. For example, I had a client who came to me after a particularly difficult interview experience. He was at first very reticent to divulge any information about 'that awful interview'. Once I gained his trust, he told me that he had never considered himself a nervous person, but once he was in the interview room the nerves took over. The questions had been firing for about ten minutes and it was then that he noticed the interview panel looking at him very strangely. It was at this point he realized that although he thought he was talking, because the words were buzzing round his head, he wasn't actually saying anything because he couldn't move his mouth. The muscles had frozen and stiffened due to extreme nerves. I have only ever come across this once. However, on working to resolve this situation, the person realized that the reason he got so nervous at interviews was because he was chasing the wrong kind of jobs. He didn't want the job he was being considered for, hence his silence at the interview. The outcome was that he realigned his career, applied for jobs he wanted, worked upon his interview performance and no longer dreaded the interview. Thus he landed himself the right kind of job.

## How to assess if you want the job

Remember that there is more to work than merely having a job. It must be a job that fulfills you and rewards you for your efforts.

So you need to assess whether this is a job that you would be proud to have, whether it offers you long-term potential and whether it is in line with your career aspirations.

## Common fears

Everyone has their own worries and concerns about attending interviews. Commonly, people may suffer from a fear of:

- meeting new people
- the attention falling on them
- travelling somewhere different
- being asked difficult questions
- failure – again
- being embarrassed or intimidated
- having to perform
- being over- or under-dressed

Knowing what gives you the jitters or wobbles means that you are halfway to resolving it; at least you know what to work on putting right. If you do not identify with any of the above points, but still get very nervous about attending interviews, work through the points on overcoming fears. It can do you no harm and may help to steady those nerves anyway.

## Calming the nerves

Calm nerves by following and practising the points listed below (see also Figure 1). At first it may seem unnatural, but with practice it will become easier.

## Calming the interview nerves

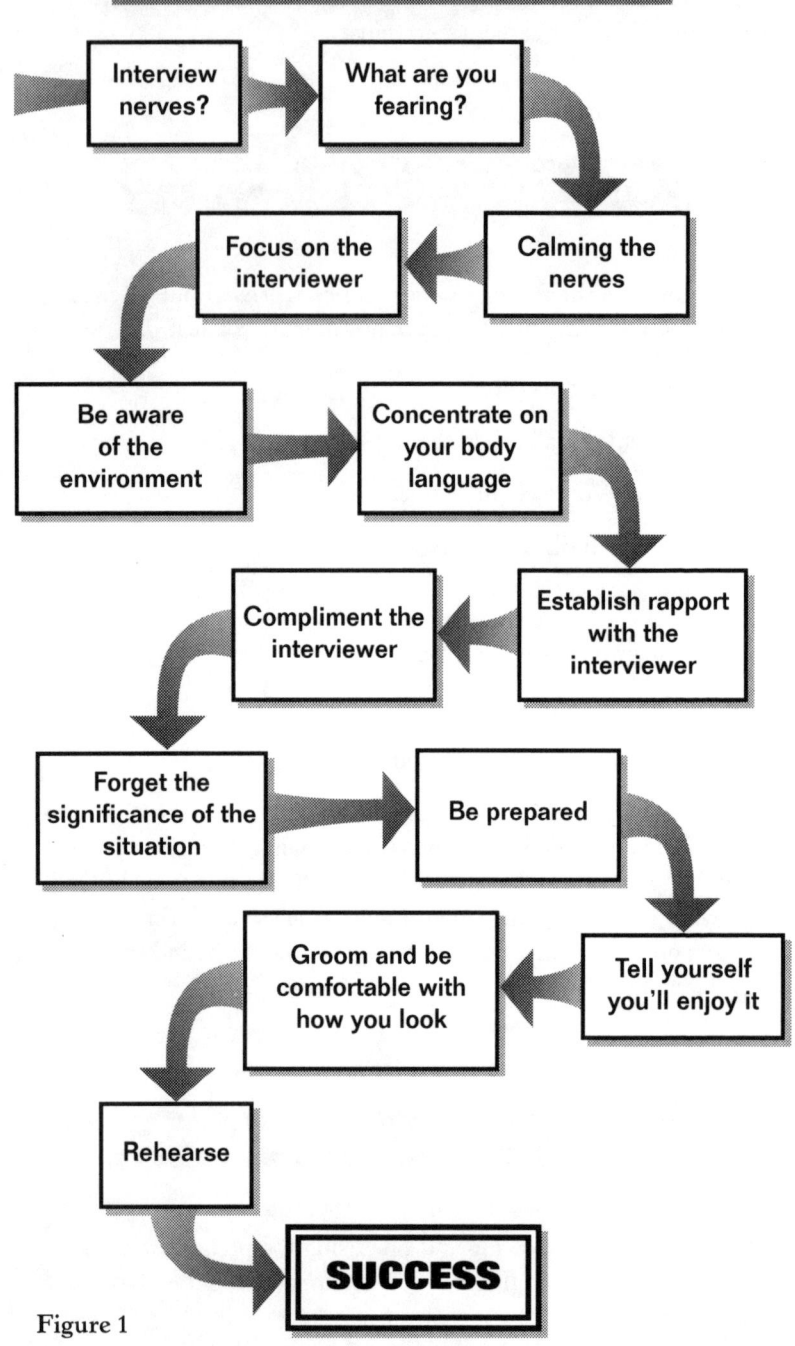

```
Interview nerves? → What are you fearing?
    ↓
Focus on the interviewer ← Calming the nerves
    ↓
Be aware of the environment → Concentrate on your body language
    ↓
Compliment the interviewer ← Establish rapport with the interviewer
    ↓
Forget the significance of the situation → Be prepared
    ↓
Groom and be comfortable with how you look ← Tell yourself you'll enjoy it
    ↓
Rehearse → SUCCESS
```

Figure 1

## HAVE FAITH IN THE SCRIPT

You wrote it, therefore it should be good! The CV or application form is the script for the interview. Everything the employer knows about you to date is written down on the paper in front of him. Before the interview, read it through several times and have faith in it. The types of questions asked will be determined by the content of the CV. Once at the interview there is *no* harm in repeating some of the information in the CV. Concentrate on the question and reply by making yourself look a winner. Focus on the positive and don't be shy. Believe in yourself and the interviewer will believe in your abilities as well. When delivering the answers sit comfortably and try not to fiddle or gesticulate. It is not necessary to go into an act, but try to make an impression upon the interviewer. Present a friendly but businesslike manner. You don't want to be locked in a permanent grin, so the occasional smile is what is required.

Above all, remember that you are in the marketplace, so sell yourself.

## FOCUS ON OTHERS

To calm the nerves, stop thinking about yourself and how you feel. This will only make matters worse, as the more nervous you feel the more nervous you will become. So, try to practise focusing on others if you feel panicky. How are the people around you behaving? While waiting for the interview, watch the people, the receptionist and the employees that you see. They are unlikely to be nervous as they are doing a normal day's work just as you usually do. On meeting the interviewer, focus on him/her rather than yourself. Listen to what he/she is saying, how he/she is coping and reacting and remember that he/she might be as nervous as you are, especially if it is the first time in the interviewer's chair.

So never underestimate other people's possible nervousness, as it will affect their behaviour too.

## BE AWARE OF THE ENVIRONMENT

Take an interest in where you are: the building you are in; the interview room; the lighting; the temperature; the decor; and also the noise level. Sometimes interviewers break the ice by asking, 'Are you warm enough?', or something similar, and too often the nervous reply is, 'I don't know'. To avoid a stupid throwaway comment that could haunt you throughout the rest of the interview, be conscious of the surroundings. Ask yourself whether you would be happy working in this environment.

## FORGET THE SIGNIFICANCE OF THE INTERVIEW

Try to forget that this is an interview. Forget the fact that you need the job to pay the bills, or that this job is a one-in-a-million opportunity, or the job of a lifetime. Thinking along these lines affects performance. It makes it difficult to concentrate and to be relaxed, and above all it increases pressure. Sportspeople often say that they try to *forget* that they are competing in the Olympics, the Wimbledon Final or the FA Cup Final. Instead they think that it is just another match, another game – the game they enjoy and live for. Do the same thing in the job interview. Forget about how you are coming over and whether you will be offered the job. Instead, concentrate on answering the questions and think about what is happening in the present. Be yourself and let your personality shine through. Don't be tempted to think about the outcome, as it will only interfere with your performance.

## TELL YOURSELF YOU'LL ENJOY IT

A positive mental attitude creates positive thoughts which turn into positive actions. Tell yourself you'll enjoy it and it will come true. It is, after all, only another business conversation, something which you have every day of your life. Learn from past mistakes and see the whole process as a learning process. Put into practice what you learned from the last interview, and remember that practice makes perfect.

## REHEARSE

It is crucial to practise being interviewed, as it will dramatically increase your performance. An interview is an unnatural set-up and can cause people to behave differently. A client of mine was totally unaware, until she saw herself on video, that once under pressure she would point and shake her finger at the person asking the questions – somewhat off-putting for the interviewer. In such a case, the interviewer might focus totally on the quirky movement rather than on what the person is saying. Are you aware of how you come across? It is common for people to wave their arms or legs, nod their head, fiddle with change in their pockets, close their eyes, or swing on the chair. Seeing yourself in action can be quite a surprise.

Practise being interviewed. Get someone you trust, either a partner or a friend, to interview you. It is best to allocate 15–20 minutes, so that the person can ask you a continuous flow of questions. This allows you to relax once the initial feelings of self-consciousness have worn off. Try to persuade the person to prepare the questions, as this makes the situation more realistic and creates the element of surprise for you. Lastly either borrow or hire a camcorder so that you can video the dummy interview.

Before looking at the tapes, get the person to give their honest opinion. Listen and take their advice, then take a look for yourself. Is this the real you on video? Watch the interview several times to allow the initial shock to wear off. You may need to do some work on your posture and your body movements. Above all, note your facial expressions. What do they tell you? Are you frowning or staring, and where is that smile? Listen to your voice. What is the pitch like? Is it flat and boring or raised and squeaky? Try to avoid falling into the habit of raising your voice at the end of each sentence, as this portrays a lack of confidence and makes it appear as if you are seeking the listener's approval to what is being said.

Subtly lowering your voice at the end of a sentence gives an authoritative and convincing touch.

## FOCUS ON YOUR BODY LANGUAGE

Adopt a relaxed, confident and motivated style of body language. In order to be relaxed, sit comfortably and relax your shoulders. Raised shoulders restricts airflow and can cause the voice to be staccato. For the women, legs should be uncrossed and kept together, with hands placed on the lap. This avoids the temptation to fidget, an obvious sign of nervousness. For men, legs can be crossed or uncrossed. If you do cross your legs, though, cross them at the ankles, as it is unattractive and off-putting for the interviewer to be faced with a hairy lower leg. With the legs being crossed at the ankle it can be helpful to squeeze them together if the pressure of interview increases. This avoids adopting defensive body language, such as folding the arms, leaning back in the chair, reducing eye contact and withdrawing from the conversation. Perhaps consider adopting a non-threatening 'query' expression, with the head on one side, slight frown and half-smile. It signals that you want to know more, but more importantly that you haven't taken offence at what the interviewer has said.

Interviewers are human too, and want to be approved of and feel comfortable with you. So a final key to successful bodytalk is to be aware of the interviewer's non-verbal signals. These are clues to your possible acceptance or rejection. You will know if you are doing well if the interviewer is interested in what you have to say – shown by leaning forward, smiling, nodding and keeping friendly eye contact. So take clues from the interviewer and copy their body language (subtly, of course).

If the interview isn't going too well, the non-verbal signals will be less positive, such as leaning back from the desk, shaking the head, tapping fingers on the desk, and avoiding eye contact. If you spot these signals, change your body language quickly and in any way you can. Either talk more or talk less, smile more or less, or use hands more or less. In short, do the opposite to what you've been doing so far. Accept that it may be too late to retrieve the situation, but nothing is lost by experimentation. It might help to tip the balance in your favour.

Lastly, it is crucial to be fully awake for your interview, especially if it's a late appointment. Increase your energy before the interview by jumping up and down in private for a few minutes. Raising the heart beat slightly increases motivation. Alternatively, if it is impossible to jig about, wake yourself up by dabbing cold water on your wrists and on the back of your neck to increase the blood flow.

Thus, signal throughout the interview that you will fit in with this company and, above all, be on your best behaviour.

## BE WELL-GROOMED AND COMFORTABLE WITH HOW YOU LOOK

Image and appearance matter. Being well-groomed shows self-respect and value for the people you meet and work with. It is not necessary to spend obscene amounts of money on the best clothes, but to buy what you can afford, to dress in accordance with the company style and to pay attention to grooming.

Dress for your interview in line with the company's image. To get it right, start by looking at the advertisement, application pack and company brochure. What image does the company portray? A glossy image might mean they want a classy, formal style; a badly photocopied pamphlet might mean that they don't pay attention to image and presentation at all. However, before forming your opinion, it is advisable to check out the company further. Before the interview, visit the building from the outside and watch the staff as they leave for lunch. If you can, go inside the building in order to get a better look. Try to pick a midweek day as some companies have a casual Friday policy. So research will show whether a suit, a creative outfit or a casual approach is required. Then customize your clothes specifically to the particular company.

A client of mine underestimated the value of a visit and as a result she missed out on the job. She modified her usual 'stand upright' hairstyle for the interview and wore more formal clothes than usual. 'It worked against me,' she told me, 'because when I arrived I realized to my disappointment that my usual hairstyle and clothing was far more in keeping with the company image. I tried to rectify my mistake by buying a can of hairspray to give my hair a bit of encouragement. Initially I thought it had worked, but then I saw myself in the mirror wearing that dreaded formal suit! I felt so uncomfortable and without doubt my lack of confidence came over in the interview. It was a shame I didn't take the advice about checking out the company in advance.'

So, if you can, do check the company out, but do it yourself, as someone else's version of 'smart' might not be yours.

## GROOMING FOR MEN

| | |
|---|---|
| **Body odour** | Ensure that you are clean and smell fresh. If in doubt, do the sniff test under the armpits. |
| **Clothes** | Wear a clean, ironed shirt. If the interview is at the end of the day, change into a clean shirt before the interview. |
| | Stick to black or blue long socks to avoid those hairy legs being seen. Choose a tie to suit and ensure that the knot is firmly into the collar. |
| | Avoid socks or ties that convey childish tendencies, for example cartoon or funny ones. It is not professional and could put the interviewer off. |
| | Press trousers the night before and avoid messy sandwich fillings on the day of the interview. |
| | Clean shoes and nails, especially if you've been gardening or doing oily jobs. |
| **Hair** | Wash hair the night before and ensure that it is combed before the interview. If you have long hair, tie it back in a ponytail. |
| | Remove all unwanted hair – especially nasal hair and hair between the eyebrows. |
| **Face** | Ensure you are cleanshaven. If you have a heavy beardline, shave again just before the interview but take care as you don't want to have a plaster stuck on your face. |

| | |
|---|---|
| General | Perhaps invest in a pocket diary and quality pen – rather than a pen with a chewed end. |

## GROOMING FOR WOMEN

| | |
|---|---|
| Body odour | Ensure that you have showered or bathed, but go easy on the perfume. |
| Clothes | Choose clothes in accordance with the company image. |
| | Avoid low-cut blouses, see-through shirts and short skirts. Your job capabilities are on show, not your body. |
| | Go easy on the jewellery. Avoid bold colours, and choose items that enhance your outfit. |
| | Check your hemline, as sometimes it can hang down at the back where a shoe has caught it. |
| Hair | Clean, tidy hair is essential, and if long tie it back. |
| | Remove any stray hairs. |
| Face | If you wish use make-up to enhance your looks – but avoid bright red lipstick and heavy eye make-up (a client revealed that he once rejected a candidate on account of her heavy make-up). |
| Shoes | Ensure that the heels are not too high. If your shoes are new, break them in beforehand, otherwise you might find yourself leaving the room with a funny walk! |

Finally, dress to be accepted, not to impress or startle the interviewer.

## ESTABLISH RAPPORT WITH THE INTERVIEWER

The interviewer will try to establish a rapport with you, but you also need to make an effort to build rapport with him/her. Many interviewees don't approach an interview in this way, preferring to adopt a passive attitude, sitting there answering whatever questions are asked to the best of their ability. Nerves can cause people to behave in this way; but it is hard work for the interviewer.

The interviewer wants you to be as interested in him/her as he/she is in you. There is nothing worse than talking to a brick wall – so don't be like one. Instead have an active approach and this will help you forget the nerves. Being active is taking control of the interview, giving the interviewer what you want to give, not necessarily what the interviewer is trying to find out. Present the facts and answers, but also inspire confidence.

It is fair to say that some people can instinctively strike up good relationships but others have to work at it. Listed below are things to consider so that rapport can be achieved between you and the interviewer.

### The initial introduction

This is vitally important. Greet the person warmly, and shake hands firmly, but don't crush the hand. A good introduction demonstrates that you are a professional, receptive person eager to provide a good service.

### Look at the interviewer

Interviewers often complain that interviewees just won't look at them. The interviewee's eyes are normally focused on the interviewer's left or right shoulder, anywhere else but the eyes. Apart from this being off-putting, the interviewer has to find out why the interviewee can't look them in the eye. If it can't be put down to initial nerves, it normally is reason for rejection.

So look, but don't stare, as this is just as disconcerting. Don't overdo eye contact. It can make the interviewer uneasy and lose track of the conversation. Indicate response by glancing down now and then and nodding to show you are absorbing what is being said.

### Have an idea of structure

This helps you to avoid repetition and hopping from subject to subject. Also the interviewer may need a bit of help if he/she runs out of ideas.

## Strike up common areas of interest

Don't underestimate common areas of interest. If you come across any, don't gloss over them. This is your chance to make the interviewer feel as if he/she is important to you. It is vital if you are to get the best out of them and to build up a good relationship. They'll tell you more, be more open and talk enthusiastically if they feel you like them.

## Listen to the interviewer

Most people won't, but you must. Remember the interviewer holds the trump card – the job offer. Your question or remarks can wait, and, if you do forget what it was, maybe it wasn't that important anyway. If it was, you can always ring up and ask at a later date. If the interviewer is happy talking, let him/her. The pressure to perform is off you. Listening means:

- not rushing the person talking to you by speeding up the interviewer's delivery, by finishing the sentence or starting your response before he/she has finished

- keeping emotional responses under control; the moment you get angry, you stop actually listening; focus on what the person is saying, not on your response

- trying to ignore distractions – don't look towards the distraction, keep your attention and focus on the interviewer

## COMPLIMENT WHERE A COMPLIMENT IS DUE

It must be an honest and genuine compliment but, if you think it, say it. Put the interviewer at ease and compliment him/her perhaps for the directions sent, the lovely location of the building, or for rearranging the appointment. Don't be shy to pass on a good word where appropriate.

## Summary

There is a lot of information to absorb here. These are all tactics that you may need to practise, but they will help to quell the nerves. Adopt some of these ideas and it will only be a matter of time before you start to enjoy being interviewed.

# THREE

# Being Prepared

Careful preparation is the route to a successful interview. Preparation avoids being taken by surprise and prevents giving away information that it would have been better to keep to yourself. This chapter deals with the types of things to prepare: working upon key subjects; understanding your strengths, weaknesses and needs; reflecting your attitude and ambitions; and promoting your skills and expertise (see also Figure 2). Thus there is more to consider than working out the odd question to ask. For once, at the interview the whole person is on view; and the interviewer is likely to want to explore certain subjects to probe and to dig deep. Preparation enables you to be open and honest and to feel comfortable with what is being asked and how you are replying. Remember that no amount of preparation will ensure you get the job, but it will ensure that your performance is your best one.

## Your attitude

Before considering how to prepare for the interview, consider first the concept of attitude, your attitude. Are you aware of your attitude during an interview? What unspoken message are you conveying to the prospective employer? I had a client that came for interview practice who felt that he needed some tips on how to be more assertive in the interview situation. 'Assertive?', I asked. He then explained how he had been promised a directorship at work, but after a row with the Chairman it had been offered to

# Being Prepared

## Interview preparation

```
Pre-interview preparation
    ↓
Sort out your attitude → Identify your ambitions
                              ↓
Prepare question topics ← Be aware of your skills and expertise
    ↓
Prepare questions to ask → Know yourself
                              ↓
                    Remember etiquette and REPLY
```

Figure 2

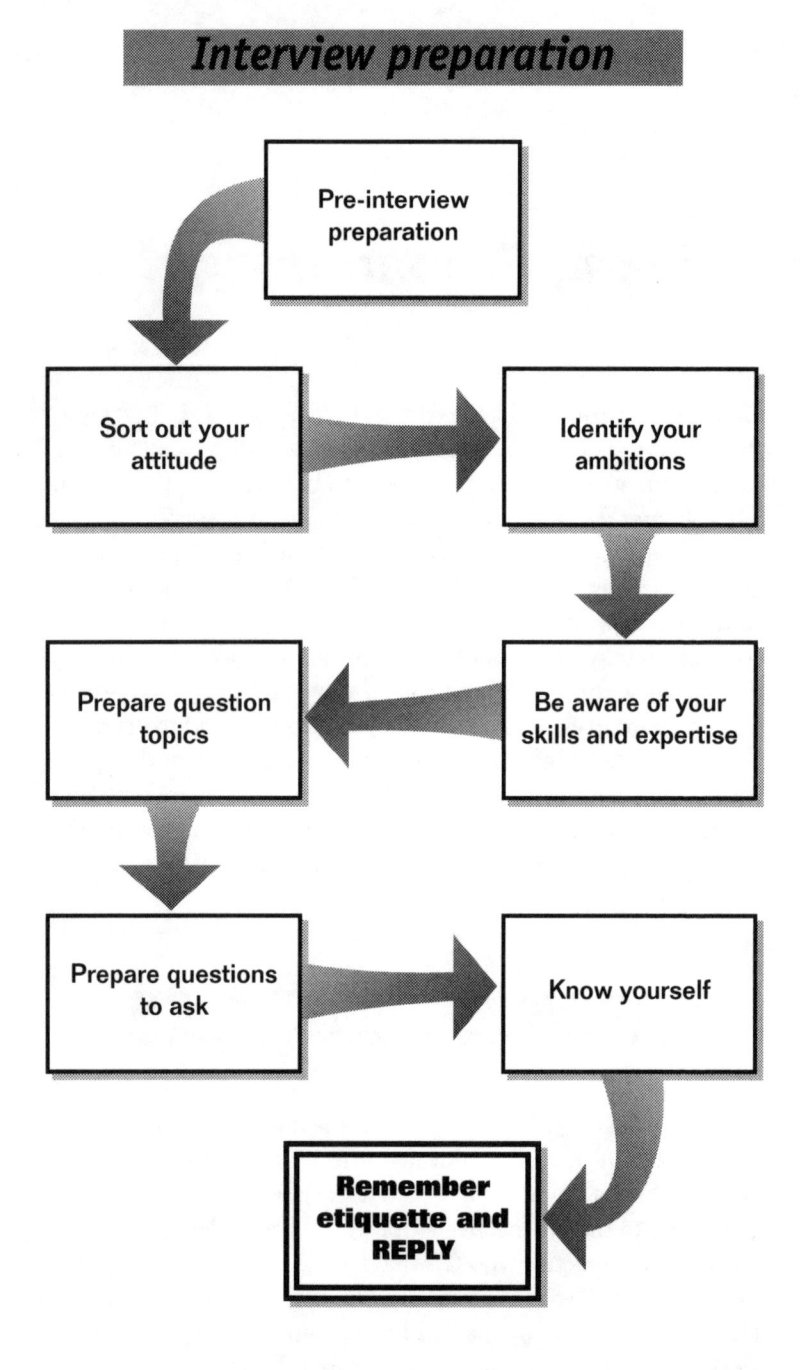

someone else. So he was now looking for an even better job elsewhere. I said to him that he seemed angry. 'Angry,' he said, 'I'm furious, it is disgusting, I am so mad about what has happened!' He *was* furious; he spoke quickly and curtly, his lip was tight and he stared hard. It was a difficult task to advise him that his anger was being taken into all interviews that he was attending, and that if he wanted to increase his success rate and ease the pressure of his current role, he had to work upon dissolving it.

Attitude is crucial to your performance. It is reflected in the tone of your CV and also in the interview. In fact, attitude speaks even louder than what you actually say. This is where most interviewees trip up, as they fail to realize the importance and significance of their attitude, the very thing that may be putting the employer off choosing them. Attitude is reflected by the choice of vocabulary, facial expressions, behaviour and dress sense. The true test of attitude is to see it in action. Have a look in the mirror or video a dummy interview. Is this the real you? Do you like what you see? On paper you may have got it right, but at an interview your facial expressions, tone, posture and movements can either confirm or conflict with what you are saying. Is your attitude making others warm to you or withdraw from you?

To make things clearer, listed below are the types of attitudes or states of mind that put employers off. Employers are not looking for a perfect candidate, because there is no such thing (although it has been said that imperfect people always want to hire perfect people). However, they are looking for a stable, realistic, positive, visionary candidate who wants a long-term future, a candidate that gives the employer more reason to say 'yes' to him/her than 'no', a candidate that will add value to the company and not one that brings all his/her baggage and problems with him/her. The interviewer has enough problems of his/her own.

However, if you do recognize yourself as adopting any of the negative attitudes listed below, then it is time for you to change. The secret to your future success is that you are now aware of the importance of attitude and if you do find yourself slipping into this type of behaviour at an interview you can amend it and quickly. The message is: if you are in the right frame of mind employers will be more attracted to you. They will then want you on their team.

## NEGATIVE ATTITUDES

### The opportunist attitude

The opportunist person has no real commitment to an employer and is liable to move on when his/her mood or requirements change. It can be detected by the interviewee giving flippant replies to questions and not talking about long-term aspirations and desires, partly because the person is as yet unsure what they are.

*Do you have an opportunist attitude?* Do you get bored easily? Do you browse through magazines and papers and only apply for jobs as and when you see something that excites you? Is it the money, car, increased responsibility or opportunities that is attracting you to apply? *Action*: You need to sort out what you want from your career in the long and short term.

### The depressive attitude

A depressive person doesn't want to take responsibility for his/her career. It can be detected by the employer because the candidate blames the company and environment for what has or has not happened. Employers will not be attracted to this person because he/she will need a lot of hand-holding and reassurance, plus he/she will affect the morale of the team.

*Do you have a depressive attitude?* Do you look for a new job when you are fed up with the one you are currently doing? Do you apply when things get on top of you at work, when you feel that you can't cope and need to escape from the monotony of your current situation? *Action:* You need to start taking charge of your career, sorting out what you want and realize that you *can* influence your situation. Think about what you enjoy doing, what motivates you and present the *good* at the interview rather than the bad.

### The angry attitude

The angry person doesn't win over the employer's approval or support. The angry person talks in terms of how the previous company should have rewarded him. A position is unlikely to be offered as his/her demands and expectations come across as being too high and volatile. Business is about fulfilling value and need and a prospective employer would question whether or not the person has exaggerated the case or has misinterpreted the previous company's promise of reward. The employer would be uneasy about employing this person in case it happened again.

*Do you have an angry attitude?* Do you start looking for jobs when you feel that you are being overlooked at work? When you notice that your colleagues and subordinates are being promoted and you are not, even though you think you should be? When you don't get the credit for a project you deserve? Or when you feel that your career is not moving as fast as it should be? *Action:* If you feel you have been unfairly treated or mistreated, beware. Talk to your boss and sort it out. You don't want to carry this disappointment with you for the rest of your career as it could grow in size with time. At an interview if the case comes up it is much better to talk about personality clashes rather than in terms of what you ought to or should have gained. Anyone can have a personality clash, and thus it is acceptable.

### The desperate attitude

Employers are proud of their company/business and want to employ people who hold similar values. Desperate interviewees are those people that see their own needs and situation as far more important than those of the employer.

*Do you have a desperate attitude?* Are you short of money and out of work? Are you threatened with redundancy? Are you unsure of what you want to do but willing to give any job a try? *Action:* You must try and see the employer's point of view as well as your own. You may find that a temporary job may ease the financial burden and pressures. You must stress your positive attributes and skills rather than saying that you will do anything, as this is too weak and feeble.

### The half-hearted attitude

Half-hearted people give themselves away because they lack stability, conviction and stamina. Employers get the impression that everything is too much effort and that they just can't be bothered. This person often refers to his/her feelings, feelings of guilt, shame and disappointment. Employers will not be attracted to this person because he/she cannot be relied upon to be self-sufficient.

*Do you have a half-hearted attitude?* Are you easily disappointed and take knocks too personally? Do you need time to heal and lick your wounds after you have been rejected? Do you give up at the first hurdle? Or do you see it as a learning process and find out the reasons you weren't selected and work on the tips you have been given? Does your job hunt lose momentum, and then you spend time feeling guilty that nothing is happening on the job front? *Action:* Work out why you are giving up. Do you really want this job?

### The emotionally unstable attitude

Employers want assurances that you will and can do the job. An employer would be concerned if you have suffered any personal or emotional problems that could affect your work performance.

*Do you have an emotionally unstable attitude?* Perhaps you have just experienced a bereavement or been through a messy divorce. If divorced or separated, explain briefly the circumstances if these add to your case. *Action:* If asked about the event, don't fall into the trap of giving the employer all the detail. He/she is not interested in this, only that you have sorted yourself out. An employer doesn't want to employ all your problems as well, as he/she has enough of his/her own.

### The know-it-all attitude

A know-it-all person doesn't warm others to his/her way of thinking. He/she is so wrapped up in his/her own self-importance and how brilliantly he/she has performed in the past that his/her attitude invites others to put him/her down or see fault in him/her. Of course, employers are interested in your previous experience but only as long as it is put in context of their needs.

*Do you have a know-it-all attitude?* Do you talk about your previous experience and assume you will do the same thing in your new role regardless? Are you open to new ideas? Do you see another person's needs and point of view? *Action:* Talk in terms of the prospective employer's needs and relate your experience to these needs.

## The irrational attitude

Irrational people give themselves away because they lack self-confidence. When asked about certain subjects, their argument falls apart and then they have an even bigger problem.

*Do you have an irrational attitude?* Are you underqualified for the job you are applying for? Are you perhaps setting your sights far too high for where you are at the moment? Are you reaching for standards that you couldn't possibly achieve right now and therefore you will always fail? Or are you applying for jobs for which you are overqualified and therefore not giving yourself a chance to reach your full potential? *Action:* Try to sort out in your own mind what you want from your career and be realistic in your approach.

## The sloppy attitude

The sloppy person either can't be bothered to get it right or isn't even aware that he/she is slipping up.

*Do you have a sloppy attitude?* Do you have a good CV and interview manner? Do you have good hygiene and appearance or are you inclined to be lax in these areas? Do you take your family circumstances into your decision-making – will this career move be a good move for just you or for the whole family? Have you considered how long hours, excessive time away from home or relocating will affect you all? The interviewer will ask you and you will be expected to have given it some thought. *Action:* Identify what the problem is, and if you don't know ask a close friend or a career advisor, or ring up the interviewer and be brave enough to ask. Try to listen to what was said and reflect upon it. Is it true or false? If false, ignore it and think no more about it, but, if true, be brave and sort it out.

## The non-conformist attitude

Employers claim that non-conformity is an automatic reason for rejection. Candidates need to demonstrate to a prospective employer that they can and will follow basic instructions and requests.

*Do you have a non-conformist attitude?* Are you letting yourself down because you are not submitting information that the employer is asking for, i.e. filling in the form badly, arriving late for an interview or giving your preferred answer to the question asked? *Action:* Whether you like it or not, remember that the only rule of job hunting is to do what the employer asks and do what you say you will do. After all, you want the job and it is not your job to criticize or change the requirements. You will have the chance to demonstrate your flair and originality at the interview and to assess whether you will fit in with the organization.

All the negative attitudes highlighted above have a higher failure rate than success rate.

## POSITIVE ATTITUDES

Employers want people to have a decisive, visionary and positive attitude, an attitude which will add value to the company. Candidates need to be aware of their capabilities, strengths and weaknesses and be able to express themselves both verbally and in writing. Remember, however, you don't have to be too slick or perfect in your approach. This in itself is often viewed as a negative attribute, because it looks too false as if you have rehearsed your performance so much that you reel if off pat, and it is therefore hard to see how much of it is you or the puppet in motion.

### A visionary attitude

A visionary approach is key to your success. It is not enough to muddle through from task to task and from job to job. Employers need conviction that you are the right person for a particular job and to convince them you need to believe in yourself first. A vision is having a clear idea of your future, your long- and short-term goals; knowing what motivates and drives you; having an awareness of your current skills and capabilities and knowing what you need to develop and learn in order to propel you forward.

If you don't know where you want your career to go, look in the papers and talk to friends, colleagues and contacts. What jobs excite you, and who do you aspire to be? You will learn to be imaginative and creative in planning your future. You will see the value of paying attention to your inner thoughts. To reach your full potential, you will need to take time to establish your vision for your career by networking, shadowing, training or using a mentor. By removing all limitations and being dedicated to your vision, you could achieve far more than you ever dreamed possible.

## A POSITIVE ATTITUDE

A positive attitude will help you to secure your success. No one wants to hire a tired, negative person; so, if you show signs of being worn down by life, sort things out. A video of a practice interview will show whether your answers are defensive or whether you are promoting yourself. If you feel positive in yourself, you will influence the environment positively and employers will want to hire you. Follow the guidelines below if you wish to create a positive attitude.

- **Take time out for yourself.** Whether it is first thing in the morning or last thing at night give yourself time off. Do things you enjoy, and remember if you build a positive attitude in one area it will spill over into another area.

- **Look for the good in yourself and others.** Nobody is perfect, but everyone has good qualities. You are a unique person and you are important. Learn to appreciate what is good about yourself. Likewise give others enthusiastic praise and appreciation. If you are jealous and bitter towards others, then be aware that this could be a sign that you wish to be like them. If you try, you can be.

- **Talk about positive things.** Positive thoughts create positive feelings and help you to build worthy relationships with others. People ask you every day 'How are you?' but the key is in your answer – is it a half-hearted one or a negative one? Convey a positive message instead.

- **Act now on your resolution.** You want action now, not in a year's time. So don't put off taking that necessary action now.

## A REALISTIC ATTITUDE

This book will help you to develop a realistic career approach and this in turn will lead to greater job satisfaction. A realistic attitude is:

- selling yourself to your highest potential.

- making those all important job and career decisions that most job hunters get concerned about.

If you set your mind to it, you can secure a job that you will enjoy, and that will enhance your abilities and your income. Thus, work can be transformed from a daily drudge into a fulfilling experience. The benefit for you is that you can have that special job rather than just fantasizing about it. Give it a try, and remember that, in order to avoid disaster and disappointment in job hunting, you have just got to keep at it and never put off until tomorrow what you can do today.

## Self-appraisal

Read the following questions and see what you have to offer an employer. Then, if appropriate, you can refer to these points in response to the interviewer's questions.

- **Are you hardworking?** Do you give your job your all or do the hours set? Do you waste time chatting or stretch out your lunch hour? Do you have tangible results to show for your efforts?

- **Are you disciplined?** What do you do in terms of meeting your tasks? Get on with it and work until you have finished? Or put things off, feel guilty about it and then complete the job in an almighty rush?

- **Are you organized?** Are you tidy or messy? Do you plan things and carry it out? Would you be able to find something somebody wanted? Or is it in a cupboard or drawer somewhere, among all the mess? Do you write things down or rely upon your memory? What about missing appointments and forgetting deadlines? Are you constantly having to do extra hours in order to catch up?

- **How good a leader are you?** Are you a born leader, inspiring others to do what you ask of them? Can you judge characters? How assertive are you? Are you diplomatic and tactful, or do you hurt others because you don't think before you speak? Are you greedy and take all the praise for a job well done, or do you share the credit?

- **What about your energy level?** Do you suffer from tiredness and have to take time to catch up on your sleep? Do you need to sleep in late on your days off in order to feel human again? Do you take regular exercise and holidays? Or do you have to phone the office when you are on holiday?

- **Are you competitive?** You want to be ahead of your peers and colleagues but do you work to achieve it? Do you constantly improve your skills? Have you got work goals which you are working towards? Perhaps a rise in salary, a promotion or a senior management role? Or are you a dreamer, hoping that someone somewhere will discover you and your attributes?

- **Are you a planner?** Do you take control and manage your own career or are you constantly hoping that someone will do this for you? Do you set goals for yourself and stick to them or do you resist any form of planning?

## Getting to the interview

There is nothing worse than being late or rushed when arriving for an interview. So plan your route in advance, allow enough time for your journey and try to arrive with a few minutes to spare in order to freshen up. If you are travelling by car, find out whether there are any road works on the route. If there are, allow extra time. If at all possible, do a dummy run beforehand and check out things like the parking facilities or location of the nearest tube station.

If you are running late take action and don't ignore it, hoping that the interviewer won't notice. He/she *will* notice and it could seriously damage your chances. Instead, be polite and when possible ring the interviewer or his/her secretary. Explain that you have been delayed and give the person an idea of your expected arrival time.

If is not at all possible to ring, perhaps because you are on a train or a plane, then remember to apologize immediately for your late arrival. This shows that you have noticed and, more importantly, that you care. In these circumstances, it is possible that the person may already be aware of your late arrival, but the apology will dissolve any irritation that they might feel.

## Planning your outfit

The key is not to dress up but to show yourself at your best. It never does anyone any harm to look well-groomed. Remember, first impressions do count. The aim is to project a positive image of yourself (see pages 42–4). The general rule is for men to stick to suits, shoes and socks, and to be well-groomed and tidy. Women should wear a suit or a dress, but not trousers, and stick to conservative jewellery and make-up. Above all, remember if you look good you'll feel good. Although you might want to be fashionable and trendy, ask yourself whether the employer would appreciate 'the look'. Dress to be accepted, not rejected.

## The acceptance letter

It is unbelievable, but most interviewees don't even bother to write to advise the employer that they will be attending the interview. Instead, they assume that the employer can read their mind. Writing an acceptance letter is necessary and is common courtesy. It demonstrates that you value the employer and the you want him/her to be as prepared for the interview as you will be. So don't forget to write an acceptance letter, because if you don't it could be a black mark against you.

## Possible interview topics and questions

Work on possible key subjects rather than on specific answers to certain questions. The danger of concentrating on answers to particular questions is that you can become flustered if something is thrown at you out of the blue. Worse still, you may fail to hear what is asked of you and just give one of your rehearsed answers anyway.

So, in order to sound natural and realistic, concentrate on key topics that are likely to crop up. Gather your thoughts and opinions and practise talking about your skills and achievements aloud. This helps avoid unnecessary stumbling, repetition and long patches of silence while you wait for inspiration to hit you. If you do find yourself lapsing into nervous behaviour, take a deep breath and wait a few seconds before restarting. Admitting that your words aren't flowing or that the question has taken you by surprise helps to ease tension on both sides and gives you the time to recompose yourself. Remember that interviewers prefer lively, non-pat answers anyway.

Questions asked tend to fall into seven basic categories. This makes preparation much easier and at least it is clear which categories need extra work. The question categories are as follows.

- Easy questions.
- Questions about you – the whole person.
- Factual or clarification questions.
- Historical questions.
- Visionary questions.
- Questions on the company and job.
- Hypothetical questions.

## EASY QUESTIONS

These questions are asked in order to put the interviewee at ease. They are normally asked between being collected and entering the interview room. These questions tend to be personal, but they are easy to answer.

- Did you find us OK?
- Did you come by train or car?
- Was it easy to park?
- Do you know this town?
- Have you been waiting long?
- Have you signed in at reception?

## QUESTIONS ABOUT YOU

There is no doubt that the interviewer will want to explore the whole person, to assess whether there is something in your background or personal/family circumstances that could affect your performance. The interviewer is not interested in all the nitty-gritty detail, but in being given assurances that you are a stable individual with a good supportive home background. So give brief and honest answers. Try to avoid taking offence that the interviewer may be probing a bit, and present your case in a positive way. The interviewer may want to explore the following areas.

- Your drive or motivation.
- Your enthusiasm, so show it.
- The number of children you have and their educational ages and abilities. Difficult personal circumstances might indicate potential outside pressures. A client of mine interviewed a 50-year-old man with very young children. My client said that it was strange, and thought perhaps it was a second marriage. The interviewee was very relaxed and said that he knew what the employer was thinking, but no it wasn't the case. 'It is just that my wife and I are what you call late starters', said the interviewee. Young children weren't a problem for the employer but he was pleased to see that the interviewee was so relaxed and at ease with his personal circumstances.
- Your marital status and the occupation of your partner (if you have one). If you have suffered a divorce or separation, it could indicate a period of depression or loss of confidence, so expect further probing. Provide assurances that the situation is in hand, and don't burden the interviewer with your problems.
- Your attitude.
- Your leisure activities.
- Your ability to mix and communicate.

Typical approaches could involve the following questions or topics.

**Start by telling me about yourself.**

An open forum, but you could so easily dig yourself into a hole. Interviewers like this approach as it breaks the ice and quickly gives them a 'gut feeling' about a person. The interviewer will have an idea about whether or not you can express yourself clearly or whether you find it difficult to find things to say. The key is not to ramble on and on. Keep it short, perhaps no more than a couple of minutes. Watch the interviewer's reaction. Is he/she bored, or listening intently to what you are saying? At the end ask the interviewer whether he/she would like you to expand further. Above all, be positive, talk about your accomplishments and make your answer relevant to the demands of the job.

**Describe your ability to cope with pressure.**

A popular topic, as jobs these days are highly demanding and pressurized. However, until you know what is expected of you in this particular job, it will be difficult for you to comment. So it is much better to ask the interviewer to clarify what he/she means and would expect of you. If you just say yes, that you can cope with pressure, you will be unable to assess after the interview whether or not this kind of pressure is for you. Your answer should give the interviewer the impression that pressure isn't a problem for you and make your assessment afterwards.

**Describe your ability to mix.**

Try to show that you can work with all kinds of people, but perhaps add that you find some people easier than others to get on with. Then expand, by explaining what you found easy and difficult in others. A good reply is, 'I have never worked for anybody I couldn't get along with.' Sometimes the question may be more specific and ask you how you cope with withdrawn or aggressive people. Before diving in and answering the question blind, it is advisable to ask the interviewer if he/she is referring to a particular individual within the company. Asking the interviewer to expand further will help you to give a specific and relevant answer rather than a waffly one.

**What are your preferred hours of work?**

Try to give a general answer, rather than saying that you like to be home by 7pm every night. However, if working late isn't a problem for you, let the interviewer know. If you don't object but prefer not to work late all the time, say so. Try to find out what the interviewer means by late, and how often it is expected. Say something like: 'I refer to late as 8pm; is this your definition of late? How often would I work late in a typical calendar month?'

### Describe your hobbies.

The employer will try to discover whether you have any leisure activities that could interfere with your work. So show that you have outside interests, but be careful of overdoing the extra-curricular activities. If you notice a photograph of something on the interviewer's desk that shows he/she enjoys the same sport as you, mention it. There is a need to demonstrate that you have interests, but not to indicate that these activities interfere with your job effectiveness. You need to strike a balance. A reasonable answer would be: 'When I get the time, I like to do ...'. A client was once put off a job because the employer stated that it was better if employees had no outside weekly commitments 'because we work late here'!

### What are your major strengths?

Difficult to answer well, but there is no time for modesty now. If you turn the question round, what the employer is really asking is, 'Do you have the confidence and skills to do this job and to do it *well?*' So relate your answer to the job in question and sing your own praises. Don't hang your head and mumble; refer to the advertisement or job description and relate your strengths to the job requirements. They might request:

- managerial skills
- technical expertise
- communication skills
- computer literacy

Choose a couple of strengths for each highlighted heading and back up your statements with examples. So, instead of saying, 'I can manage people', try saying something like, 'I adopt a varied style of management dependent upon the situation. For example, if the need arises I will and can discipline individuals, but in other instances I might choose to lead by example or to enlist the support and help of the team and to come to a group decision. 'I have high standards for myself and I can motivate and encourage others so that they too perform at their best.' Expect the interviewer to probe and to dig deep. You may be asked, 'How did you achieve something?' or 'What was the benefit of this or that?' Thus, the key is to remember you are in charge, so only offer truthful and relevant information.

### What are your weaknesses?

Undoubtedly this question will be asked. It shows a lot about how you perceive yourself. Avoid answering, 'I don't have any', because everyone has faults and is not proud about certain things about themselves. It is best to keep your answers short – and to the point. The interviewer isn't interested in graphic details about the case, who said what and the effect on you. Don't try to justify yourself and seek approval from the interviewer. It won't be given.

The key is to turn a weakness into a strength. For example your weakness might be *impatience*. If this is the case, you could say that, 'I get impatient with people who go home when they haven't finished the job'. Other weaknesses, such as *disappointment*, *failure to understand*, or *lack of acceptance*, could be described as follows. 'I get disappointed with people who are rude and bad mannered. I respect everyone I work with.' 'I fail to understand when people are deliberately destructive or sloppy because I love and take pride in what I do'. 'I find it hard to accept when people don't take responsibility for what they've done, because I will.'

## FACTUAL OR CLARIFICATION QUESTIONS

These questions tend to be about you and are used to clarify things on the CV or application form. They tend to only need a one-line answer, but they are asked in order to gain more information on you.

- Do you drive?
- Do you smoke?

- How would you feel about relocating?
- How long have you been at your current address?
- Are you in good health?
- Have you ever had any serious health problems?
- Are you married?
- What made you choose to do ...?

## HISTORICAL QUESTIONS

These questions concentrate on your past academic record and work experience. Highlight key points, talk about what you enjoyed, and what you are good at. The types of questions asked might be academic or job-related.

### Academic

- What subjects did you do for your degree, A levels, O levels?
- What did you enjoy about .... subject?
- How did doing these .... subjects benefit you?

### Job-related

- **What are you responsible for in your job?** Be brief and stress your strengths.

- **What did your last appraisal highlight?** It is not enough to say, 'I got an excellent appraisal'. You need to highlight the good aspects and also describe the areas that need to be developed.

- **I am concerned about your lack of…** Never be intimidated by this, because its a good sign. It means that the person is generally interested but has a reservation or two. (I can see where you might be concerned about that but all I've been doing really for the past two years is ….)

- **You have been out of work for a long time.** Say something along the lines of: 'In an ideal world I would have preferred it not to have happened but I put my time to good use.' Also give a hint, though, that it has been a tough time for you. Perhaps mention that you enjoy being busy and working, therefore it was hard work being unemployed.

- **You have had a lot of jobs in your career. Why?** Again, don't deny this. The interviewer is primarily concerned about your loyalty and stability and will want to find out if there is any underlying reason for it. Try to back up the reasons for moving. Perhaps your partner or spouse had a mobile job, or perhaps you chose a career that encourages development by moving a lot. Try to demonstrate that you have been stable for a number of years now. *But* never blame others for your instability, as it clearly gives the impression that you are not in charge of your career or life.

- **You have been with the same company for a number of years, so how will you cope with a new company?** The employer wants assurances that you are not running away from something, and that you haven't got bored. The employers want assurances that you are ambitious. Show how you grew and built up your experience with your last company, rather than that you got stuck there. Show adaptability by having worked in a number of environments and for a number of people. The key is to demonstrate that loyalty is an asset, not a liability. Perhaps you might want to express something along the lines of, 'I am an achiever and a committed person not a person who will be here today, gone tomorrow. I give a job my all.'

- **Your salary is quite low?** If you agree, try to express something positive rather than saying, 'So you see why I am leaving.' Perhaps express that it is a difficult balance between enjoying what you do with what you get paid.

- **What are your dislikes about the current job?** Be conscious that this is where your attitude is exposed. If you are angry, dissatisfied or disheartened it will come across. So if you have any kind of grievances try to reconcile these beforehand. You need to say that on the whole the job has fulfilled you – otherwise you may be asked why you have been there for ten years. Talk about general issues – the fact that you have outgrown it, or that the job now lacks challenge or that the company is no longer expanding as fast as it once was. Where necessary, back up statements with facts and figures to give the employer a true reflection of what you are saying.

- **What do you like about your current job?** Try not to present too rosy a picture, otherwise the employer may think that you can stay there! Again talk in general terms about the philosophy of the business, the product or the people. You might say that it is in your nature to try to get on with everyone you work with, and to input a lot of effort into building trustworthy business relationships. So try to ensure that your likes aren't too specific to your present organization but that they are transferable likes.

- **Why do you want to leave your current job?** Never hide things, because you will be found out. If you have been made redundant, never make excuses and never make yourself out to be a victim either. 'There were a lot of organizational changes. I have no hard feelings. I learned a lot and I am ready for a change.' Be honest and always try to turn a negative situation into a positive one.

- **What part of the job was the easiest/hardest?** Always show what experience you have gained.

- **What would you say you contributed most to your last job?** Give yourself the credit, but don't go over the top! Try not to exaggerate or make something sound more impressive than it really was.

- **Which aspects of your last job do you feel will help you in this job?** Answer briefly and honestly.

- **How much authority did you have in your last job?** Where possible, back up your statements with facts and figures to give the interviewer an indication of your power. For example, 'My budget was £...?'

- **What was your general impression of your last employer?** Above all, be positive and stress what you have gained rather than all your frustrations. If you have had differences, it is best not to mention these as you don't want to be drawn into any discussions about them. Talk about the philosophy of the company and the people.

### VISIONARY QUESTIONS

These questions focus on the future, i.e. your future. The employer wants to ascertain what ideas and aspirations you have for your career, if any. Where do you want to be within an organization, what do you want to be doing, and for whom? These questions could throw you off guard unless you have given them some thought. These questions also give you an indication of how well you are performing. A lot of emphasis could mean that the employer is really interested in you and your future with them, especially if the questions become quite specific. However, don't despair if only one or two are asked because if your answers have been specific and carefully thought out it may leave little else for the employer to ask.

### What are your future long-term career plans?

Avoid going off on a tangent and try and relate your answer to the organization in question. 'I see myself doing...more management or operating at board level – shaping and directing the company.'

### What do you expect to be doing and earning in five years' time?

This is a far more specific question. It is not advisable to answer by saying, 'Your job.' People can find this quite threatening, especially if they have no plans to move on. Talk about skills and expertise you want to gain and be exposed to over the next five years. In terms of salary, beware. Quote a 'five-year-hence salary figure' with care. It is much better to quote high and have to justify (i.e. percentage per annum plus promotion and hypothetical increase) than to quote too low a figure. The employer will divide the difference between your quote and present salary by five to represent the increase per year, and this may be much below your aspirations. Remember there is always a premium for starting salary above present salary if the employer really wants you. Read the five-year-salary question to mean, 'Are you going to stick with us for a while and then jump somewhere else?' Answer something like, 'I like what I do and I see myself doing more and doing it better.'

## QUESTIONS ON THE COMPANY AND JOB

These questions give a clear indication of your enthusiasm and desire for the job. The employer has ensured that he has prepared for the interview, but should the interviewee bother? Don't try to get away with avoiding this area of preparation, because if you really want to work for the company you will be expected to know something about them. The questions might be as follows.

- **What do you know about us?** Make sure you know the answer. If you are applying for a job through an agency ensure that you have some information on the client, and if you are applying direct do your research.

- Who are our competitors?
- Why do you want to work for us?
- How long will you be satisfied in this job before you seek promotion?
- What kind of contribution could you make to this firm?
- What reservations do you have about the job?
- Do you know anyone that works here?
- **What interests you about this job?** Avoid saying 'Money', otherwise you will be eliminated. Even though you may be desperate for this job, don't say this. Play the game. The interviewer is probing to see how much research you have done. Say what company brochures you have read and what appealed to you – the Chairman's philosophy, ideas for the future. Avoid personal considerations such as the company being near to your home, the salary being high, the perks, or the fact that your partner found the job for you. Instead, show that you are an ideal person for the job and indicate why working for the company would be stimulating for both parties.
- **You have too much experience for this job, so why do you want it?** Having too much experience is not a problem. Thank the interviewer for his/her compliment. 'It's nice of you to say that, but I don't see it as a problem.' Perhaps say something along the lines of: 'I'd rather go into a new job with a lot of experience than with little.'
- **What is your opinion of this company?** Whatever you do, don't be tempted to criticize even though it might be justified. It will not be appreciated and the effect for you will be disastrous. If you know people that already work there, without name-dropping, mention that contacts have told you this and that. Another good answer might be that you haven't had

much of a chance to draw any real conclusions, but what you have seen you are impressed with. Finally, finish by adding that you could make a valuable contribution because of this and that.

- How would you tackle the problems we have described?

## HYPOTHETICAL QUESTIONS

These are perhaps the most difficult of all. They probe your depth of experience, your ability to cope and to see how you think on your feet. Try to view them as positive questions, for the employer wouldn't waste time asking these *unless* he/she is really interested in you. He/she is ensuring that you fully meet the criteria and pressures of the job. Don't be worried to take a little time to think about it, but tell the employer you are doing this, otherwise he/she might read your reaction in a negative way. Be open and honest and ready to answer why you would adopt such-and-such an approach. The employer will test you to see if you will stand by your decision, which is vital. Don't feel pressurized to change your mind. Tell the employer that you can see his/her point, but indicate the benefits of your approach. Examples of questions asked may be:

- What you would do in such-and-such a situation?
- How would you deal with such-and-such a person?

If you don't have the benefit of drawing upon personal experience, never make some up. Say that you haven't actually had to deal with such-and-such a situation, but if it did happen you would do this – or tell the employer about a similar incident first and then say how you resolved it. Thus, always ensure that the case has a positive outcome rather than a disastrous one!

The questions asked will tell you a lot about the prospective employer, for example the philosophy of the company, the level of commitment required by employees, the emphasis on career or succession planning and the style of management. The time and emphasis given to each of these questions will help you form your opinion about the company.

## Final pre-interview checklist

- Check the interview time and date. It is not uncommon for interviewees to misread the letter, so take another look.

- Are you aware of your attitude/state of mind? Get in the right frame of mind and ensure you portray your best side.

- Have you prepared the topics that are likely to crop up? Do any last-minute preparation now.

- Are you aware of the different types of questioning styles?

- Plan your outfit and route.

- Have you got a copy of your CV or application form with you? Read through the forms one last time to remind yourself of content and emphasis.

- Have you got a phonecard and small change with you in case you run late?

- Have you done your homework on the background of the company?

- Do you have some questions you want to ask?

- You are now ready for action – good luck.

# FOUR

# Asking Constructive Questions

You will be invited to ask questions of your own at some stage during the interview. Usually, your question time is at the end, and in some circumstances interviewees are actually told to keep *all* questions until the end. This keeps the interview structure and stops the interviewer jumping from subject to subject. Interviewers expect you to ask questions, but don't be tempted to think you have to be clever, funny or impressive – you don't. Use this time as an opportunity to be a detective, to find things out about the company, the job and your predecessor. It is your chance to gather information in order to help you make a calculated and informed decision, should you be offered the job. In fact, the interviewer and the company are now in the spotlight. You are scrutinizing them. This chapter will show you the right kinds of questions to ask and which questions to avoid at all costs.

## Question types

The questions the interviewee asks, like the interviewer's questions, reflect a lot about the candidate, i.e. personality, attitude and thinking of the person. It is, therefore, advisable to *think* about not only the question itself but also its underlying message. For example, the interviewee's questions give the employer an indication of:

- how well the person listens.
- how much input the person likes to have.
- how inquisitive or forward-thinking the person is.
- the person's attitude.
- how active or passive the person is.
- how company- or 'self'-orientated the person is.

Listed below are the types of questions that you could ask to demonstrate the above points.

## LISTENING

It is vital for interviewees to show that they can listen to others, to show that they can assimilate what is said in order to be able to act upon instructions, and, where necessary, make decisions based on their findings. So, when your question time arrives, think before you speak. Don't ask a question just for the sake of asking something. Also, try to avoid asking a repetitive question, otherwise the interviewer will wonder whether you have been asleep or whether you are just stupid. Instead, show that you have been listening, reflect back some of the things that have been said, and tag your question on the end. For example, use phrases like:

- I noticed you said ...
- I believe you mentioned ...
- You stated that the company achieved ...

and then add on a question, such as:

- So how was that resolved?
- How was that inputted?
- What influence did the person performing the job have?

## INPUT

Everyone wants and likes a different level of input into a job. Try to reflect the type of input, freedom or direction you seek by asking specific questions.

- How receptive is the company to new ideas?
- How influential would you expect the person to be?
- How much of a free reign will the person have?
- How much of the philosophy and direction on the company is driven by Head Office?
- How open-minded is the company?
- How much flexibility would the person have?
- How much influence would the company want?

## INQUISITIVE AND FORWARD-THINKING

It is important to demonstrate to the employer that you have a certain amount of drive, ambition and commitment. How much you reveal is up to you but the following examples demonstrate a range of possibilities.

- What policy does the company have on promotion?
- How receptive is the company to training and the acquisition of new skills?
- How are employees picked for promotion?
- How is training financed?
- How are appraisals conducted in this company?
- How is training given in-house or externally?
- What are the prospects for this job?

- What is the next step after this job?

In order to assess the suitability of your own skills and expertise, you might want to ask more specific questions about the job and personality of the desired candidate. It is advisable to tread carefully and to ask the questions in a non-threatening way.

- I am curious to know what made the company look externally to fill this position.
- What have been the major achievements of the previous incumbent within this role? (The answer will give an indication of the level of expertise required to perform the role well; the profile of the role; and the image and attitude of the company towards the successful or perhaps less successful person who once had this job.)

Specific questions to ask about the company and job could be:

- What do you see as the major objectives of this role?
- What is the number one priority for the person taking this job?
- What is the company's mission statement?
- Is this a newly formed role or an old one?
- What expectations do you have for the person taking the job?
- What is the hardest thing to achieve in the role?
- What is the profile of the role?

## ATTITUDE

Having the right attitude is key to any appointment. The pitfalls that many interviewees fall into are shown in Chapter 3. However, it is often a case not of what they say but of how they put their message across. Below are some guidelines to help you avoid the common mistakes.

- **Humble yourself.** To do this you may need to give the employer the power by saying something along the lines of 'You may not want to answer this question but how ...', or you could use a more direct expression by saying, 'I know I am being curious/nosy or cheeky but ...'. It is a useful technique to use especially if you have difficult questions to ask. The effect is phenomenal. The interviewer will normally respond by giving you the information you require partly because you have shown deep respect for him/her.

- **Avoid challenging the interviewer.** Throw out the 'why' question, because interviewers don't want to explain or justify themselves to interviewees. Instead use how or what questions. These are less threatening and demonstrate your interest rather than aggression.

- **Never say 'I want' or 'I expect'.** It sounds simple but it can be an easy thing to slip up on especially if you get over-confident. Use instead the conditional tense as it is a much softer approach, for example, 'If at all possible, I *would* prefer' or 'It *would* be nice *if*'.

- **Be positive and constructive.** Avoid expressing a negative opinion in the form of a question. It will grate and could aggravate the interviewer. If at all possible say, 'I liked the way you do such and such here and I was wondering whether if I was offered the job such and such would be possible?'

## ACTIVE OR PASSIVE

Employers want active rather than passive employees. To show that you are an active person, prepare and ensure that you ask the interviewer some questions. It is rare that all of your questions will have been answered but, if your mind goes blank, give yourself some extra thinking time by saying that you were going to ask about...and then list the topics that have already been discussed. Then, either the interviewer will offer more information or your prepared questions will suddenly spring to mind.

A passive approach is just to sit there and say that everything you wanted to know has already been answered. If interviewees adopt a passive approach, employers could interpret this in a negative way, for example that the person accepts things too easily, or that the person doesn't really want the job because he/she hasn't thought about it in any depth and doesn't want to ask about its opportunities, prospects or profile.

So avoid being passive. Instead show your enthusiasm for the job and tell the employer that you are interested and excited about the job. Tell the employer that you want this job. Then talk about the job being yours. To do this, when you ask the questions say, 'If I was offered the job ...'.

## COMPANY-ORIENTATED OR SELF-ORIENTATED

Employers want to see that employees have the company's interests at heart, not their own. Employers know that interviewees are interested in the terms and conditions of the job, but they don't want this to be their primary and only consideration. So try to avoid the 'self' questions at all costs – the questions that shout loud and clear, 'What am *I* getting out of this job?' In summary, don't ask specific questions that refer to your needs, wants and desires.

Questions to avoid are:

- When would *I* start?

- Can *I* see *my* office?

- Can *I* smoke in the office?

- *I* want to do an MBA; would this be possible?

- How much would *I* earn?

- What social activities and facilities does the company provide for *staff*?
- What would *my* company car be? At the moment I drive a ....
- How many staff would *I* have?
- *I* like to work flexi-time; do you?
- *I* like to leave on time; would that be possible?

The 'self' questions don't add to your case. In fact, they could undo all the hard work that has been done so far. However, it is possible to get around this hurdle by asking many of these questions in terms of the company's needs, wants and desires. For example, you could ask 'When would the company like the person who is offered the job to start?' or 'What is the company policy on smoking/flexitime?' or 'What is the company policy on training such as MBAs?' The interviewer will then give you the answer and will normally turn the question round and ask you whether you have considered doing such a course. It is then possible to enter a general, open and honest discussion where you express your desire to do it but you pitch your answer according to the interviewer's attitude to the qualification.

As well as discovering more about the job, try to show an understanding for the job and the company's needs. Typical questions are:

- **What performance would the company expect of me, if I was offered the job?** At least you can establish whether these expectations are high or low and, more importantly, achievable.

- **What are the main strengths that the company is looking for in the successful candidate?** You can then assess later whether these strengths are in your repertoire. Remember, show respect for the company and the interviewer will respect you.

- **What is the company's attitude to change?** You can assess from the answer what the company has achieved to date, how receptive the organization is to change and how this fits in with your ideas.

## Tips to remember

A number of tips on asking questions are listed below to help you avoid the pitfalls.

- **Time.** Be conscious of time and watch the interviewer's reactions while you are talking. Is the interviewer listening to what you are saying or trying to speed up your delivery by fidgeting, clock-watching or interrupting? Remember you only have a limited amount of time to ask questions, so don't ramble on and on. Value the interviewer's time and give him/her an idea of the number of questions you want to ask. Between 5 and 10 is a reasonable number, but beyond that you are pushing your luck.

- **Trust your memory.** It is much better if you ask a question from memory rather than dragging out a scrappy bit of paper and reading out your questions. Talking from memory will create an informal atmosphere and the interviewer's response will be more genuine.

- **Single questions only.** Avoid multiple and confusing questions. Keep your questions simple and logical. Use how, what, when and where, rather than why, to ensure that the reply is informative and detailed.

- **Avoid comparing the answer.** Once the interviewer has given his/her answer to your question, avoid passing comment. For example, many interviewees think that it is their place to say, 'Oh, we did that at my previous company', or even offering a contradictory comment such as, 'Oh, we don't do that at my current company but this ...'. Interviewers say that they find this approach irritating and annoying. A client advised me, 'I get so tired of hearing how other companies are run and how they do this and that. I am tempted to say, 'Well, if you prefer the way your company does business then stay there!'

# FIVE

# Dos and Don'ts

This chapter contains a list of interview dos and don'ts. Some of the points listed below may have been mentioned in previous chapters, but they are all worth repeating and remembering. Read the lists before an interview, as it a useful way of refreshing the memory.

## Essential requirements

**Do be yourself.**

Perhaps the most important *do* of all is to be yourself. Don't try to adapt, modify or change your behaviour as you could end up making yourself look a fool. The interviewer is interested in learning about you, the whole person. Your personality is as important as your background. Don't be afraid of demonstrating your sense of humour, your enthusiasm or your logical manner – all the qualities that make you special.

**Do concentrate on the question.**

The question has been asked, so answer it as best you can. Avoid waffling or getting away from the point as you risk boring the interviewer. If you are unsure of whether you have answered a question fully, ask. Then, if need be, expand in greater detail.

Answer the questions using the term 'I' rather than 'one'. 'One' is pompous and artificial and reserved for the privileged few. Also, if you do use 'one', you could end up being a bit tongue-tied after a while.

**Do always tell the truth.**

The truth is good enough, so stick to the facts. Don't fall into the trap of trying to make something sound more impressive by exaggerating. If there are any gaps in your CV or failed exams, don't be embarrassed, but explain the situation honestly and precisely; try to show, however, that you have learnt from the experience. It is much easier to remember what you have said if you tell the truth. Telling the truth means that you will build trustworthy relationships.

**Do be positive, enthusiastic and interesting.**

Be positive throughout the interview. Resist the temptation to be picky or critical; this will only reflect back upon you. Remember that enthusiasm generates energy and positive feelings in the listener. So, talk enthusiastically about your current role and previous jobs. The tone of your voice is a real indication of what is being said. Vary the pace and also the pitch to keep the listener interested and alert.

**Do read the clues.**

Just as you should be conscious of your posture, facial expressions and body movements, watch the interviewer's body signals. Take the clues you are being given. If the signals are positive, don't cut the interviewer down, but if the clues are negative wrap up what you are saying and change your tactics quickly.

**Do be loyal.**

Don't be tempted to moan about previous jobs, bosses and management style. Personality clashes are acceptable, but long moans aren't. Minimize discussions of this sort and stress something positive. Above all, show that you put the interest of the supervisor, associates and company before your own.

### *Do* arrive on time.

If you arrive too early it could be interpreted that you are an over-anxious type of person. If you are late you could be labelled as being arrogant. So, the best advice is to arrive on time. Allow adequate travelling time and time to prepare yourself beforehand.

### *Do* be well-mannered.

Take clues from what you hear, but if in doubt refer to the interviewer as 'Mr/Mrs or Ms'. Be courteous and thank people for their time and efforts on your behalf.

### *Do* your homework.

Never, never attend an interview without doing your preparation beforehand. If you don't prepare, the interviewer will wonder what else you can't be bothered to do.

### *Do* look your best and follow the company dress code.

Well, you want to be accepted, don't you?

### *Do* make eye contact.

Eye contact is vital, but don't stare.

### *Do* smile.

The face portrays emotion. So, although you might say that you are happy with the job, the interviewer won't believe you unless your face supports this. So, smile occasionally, but don't grin.

### *Do* listen.

Listen, and listen throughout the whole interview. Answer what has been asked, not what you want to tell the interviewer. Don't interrupt the interviewer and keep emotions under control.

### *Do* establish rapport.

Build a rapport with the interviewer and don't ignore common areas of interest.

### Do know what happens next.

If nothing is said, ask; otherwise you could be hanging on for ever and ever.

### Do choose the right kind of food.

If it is a lunchtime or evening interview in a restaurant, choose food that is easy to eat and not too messy. Also, make sure that you will be able to talk through the meal. So many people, when faced with food, give the food their attention and neglect the people around the table. Also be conscious of what you order. Take the lead from the interviewer, as it is not polite to use this as an opportunity to 'pig out' or to choose very expensive items from the menu. Remember, the conversation is your major priority, and the food secondary.

### Do say you want the job.

No one expects you to beg, but if you want the job then say so – for example, 'This is a job that I would be pleased to accept'. So many candidates fail to show their enthusiasm and therefore leave the interviewer in doubt about their thoughts on the job. Apply pressure but don't try to force an offer out of the company by asking whether or not you will be selected. Be keen, but not pushy.

### Do have an answer.

Interviewers sometimes ask interviewees, 'If you were offered the job, would you accept it?' I was horrified at an interviewee who responded by saying, 'Well, I want to discuss it with my wife. She may not want me to take the job, and she may think of something I haven't thought of, so I need to think about it.' The interviewee didn't think about the implications of his answer. The interviewee confirmed to the interviewer that he was not a suitable candidate because his wife was pulling the strings, not the interviewee himself.

Instead, give a positive answer. Say what you like and what you would enjoy and, if you don't want to commit yourself, say that it would be a job you would thrive on. Above all, ensure that you convey that you are in charge of your career and you are not someone else's puppet.

## Pitfalls to avoid

***Don't* take someone else into the interview.**

Leave your wife, husband, partner, mum, dad, brother, sister or any other emotional crutch (for example, the dog) at home, or at least outside the building. It is you who is being considered for the job, not the whole family.

***Don't* disguise ignorance.**

It is much better to say that the question is unclear than to dig yourself into a hole.

***Don't* read sinister meanings into innocent questions.**

Remember no one is out to get you, so relax. The interviewer wants you to perform well. Sometimes clients of mine have expressed anger at having to write something down at an interview. A typical explanation for their anger is: 'Well, he was out to trip me up. It was obvious that he wanted to have my handwriting analysed!' Of course this is possible, but it is highly unlikely. Paranoia of this kind should be avoided at all costs, as it will only affect your performance. Try not to take things personally. Concentrate on the task in hand and just ensure that the handwriting is neat and legible. Then think no more about it.

***Don't* lose interest in the interview.**

You may realise halfway through the interview that you have made a mistake because the job on offer isn't the job for you. Don't switch off, be flippant or ask to leave. Behaving in this way could prejudice your chances of being considered for another job with the same company. If the job is offered to you, you can always turn it down, or if you are invited to attend a second interview you could write to withdraw your application.

***Don't* smoke.**

You may be desperate for a cigarette but resist the temptation, even if the interviewer is smoking. Smoking will distract your attention and shows nervousness. Also, it is not unheard of for interviewees to light up the curtains or carpet.

### *Don't* over-drink.

If the interview is taking place over lunch or in the evening, be careful what you drink. Always order what you are used to and *never* drink to excess. If you don't want to drink alcohol, order something soft but don't make an issue out of it.

### *Don't* wear strange items of clothing.

Never wear outdoor clothing for an interview. Similarly, don't wear sunglasses, hats or gloves. Leave coats and baggage in the waiting room.

### *Don't* embarrass the interviewer.

Remember the higher up the organization you get the more nervous the interviewer will be, because he doesn't do it that often. So try to put him/her at ease. Avoid being a threat to the interviewer and be careful when asking technical questions. Avoid *pushing* for detailed technical answers because the interviewer may not have all the answers to hand. Ask general questions, so that the interviewer can be as specific as he/she likes.

### *Don't* tell jokes.

The interview is not the place for joke-telling, but it is worth showing that you have a sense of humour.

### *Don't* be coarse.

Avoid chewing gum, sucking sweets or using foul language. It won't impress anyone.

### *Don't* name-drop.

Who are you trying to impress? Avoid referring to all the celebrities that you know. Also never call someone a friend unless they actually are one, because you could be caught out.

***Don't* criticize.**

You may be right, of course, but now is not the time to score points. Avoid criticizing the interviewer, company and others, as it will *only* reflect back on you. Remember that we tend to notice in others faults that we have ourselves.

Above all remember that your performance doesn't have to be perfect but it should be your best one.

# SIX

# Closing the Interview

There is an old saying that the close is as important as the opening. Often interviewees don't place that much emphasis on the close because relief enters into the equation – relief that 'the whole ordeal' is nearly over. Save the relief for afterwards and maintain concentration until the very end of the interview; then you won't slip up or make a mistake right at the end.

A client once told me that his most embarrassing moment was at a job interview.

> 'I was being interviewed for a fabulous job. I had done so well, or so I thought. I hadn't had any difficulty with any of the questions and I had done a great sales pitch. I was overcome with emotion when I heard the interviewer say, "Well, thank you very much for your time. I have asked you everything I want to ask you." On hearing these words, my legs sprang into action and I jumped up. I shook the surprised interviewer by the hand and made for the door in earnest. Once through the door I thought how strange it was that it was so dark outside. It was only then that I realized that in my haste I had chosen the cupboard door and not the exit!'

So endings are important. By this stage most interviewees are completely relaxed and their defences are down. Thus, the interviewer has a glimpse at the 'real person's behaviour and character'. The interviewer can then make an assessment as to whether the relaxed person is the same as the 'person who has been on show for the whole of the interview'.

The following are a few tips on how to close an interview successfully.

## TALK SLOWLY

There is often a great temptation to rush the last bit, but don't. Often interviewees are rushed because they have another appointment to get to. Try to avoid this if you can, because it won't reflect too well on you. It can look as if your outside activity, lunch date or wherever it is you are off to is uppermost in your mind. This may not be the case but you don't want to give the interviewer this impression, or that you can't manage your time. So, reschedule another appointment and allocate your full time and attention to this one.

Instead, take your time to come to a satisfactory conclusion, choose your words and speak slowly. If you have forgotten to ask or say something, now is your chance to do so.

## BE SENSIBLE

It is a fact that people often remember the last thing a person has said. A throwaway or silly remark could leave the interviewer in doubt about you. So, remain professional and say something that will leave the employer with a favourable impression of you. The way to do this is to use the summarizing technique and to reflect back some of the things that have been discussed (see page 19). Firstly, talk about the employer/interviewer's *need*. For example, you could say something along the lines of: 'My understanding from what has been said is that you *need* a person who can manage people effectively; a person who is technically proficient; an ambitious and highly motivated individual; and a person who will be committed to the development of the business.' In this way, reflect back what has been said in order to demonstrate that you have been listening throughout the interview, not just talking at the interviewer. The next step is to do a final sales pitch on yourself. Tell the employer how you can fulfil his/her need. To do this, summarize your key strengths and assets. Don't be afraid to be bold, and remember this is your last chance. So, perhaps, say something like, 'I feel that I have the experience and expertise to fulfil your need. I would draw upon ...', and then briefly list your key relevant strengths.

It is a powerful technique that will make you stand out from the rest of the competition. It demonstrates your professionalism, self-belief and above all your self-confidence. It leaves the interviewer with a truly positive impression of you. Give it a try and see how it can work in your favour.

## ASK WHAT HAPPENS NEXT

It is a good idea to be aware of the next steps. To do this, ask the employer whether any action is required from yourself. If there is something for you to do, make sure you do what you have promised to do. To avoid waiting anxiously for the post every day, ask when you can expect to hear about the job.

## THE FAREWELL

End the interview by shaking hands with the interviewer and by thanking them for their time. If it is appropriate you may want to ask to have a 'walk' around the premises. This might convey your real interest. You may have to wait in another room to be told whether or not you have been selected. Most probably you will be contacted by letter within the next couple of days. Until then, relax. You can do nothing to influence the interviewer's decision now. Some people like to write a thank-you letter. If you choose to do this, make it brief. Express your thanks for the interviewer's time and stress your wish to work for the company. A letter is a thoughtful gesture, but normally it won't affect the decision. That will have already been made, with luck in your favour.

# SEVEN

# Alternative Interviews

The alternative interview doesn't mean alternative attitude or behaviour. The alternative interview can take the form of a group interview, test, telephone interview or presentation. It is an alternative style of interviewing that is usually followed by a one-to-one interview. Here the interviewer can question the person further on the findings of the alternative interview. Alternative interviews are designed to show much more about the individual than the ordinary structured interview. Selectors choose this approach because it is quicker and offers greater flexibility to do the following:

- to screen the applicants.
- to assess whether the person will fit into the organization.
- to test the person's abilities.

Every organization which uses the alternative interview will have a different specification and reason for adopting this method of selection. On the whole, selectors use this style of interviewing because they want to see the candidate's skills in action rather than in the passive state. Listed below are typical characteristics and abilities that selectors may wish to assess in *all* of the interviewees. Sometimes interviewees are awarded marks according to their performance and offers are then made on the basis of these marks. Usually, however, it is a combination of the one-to-one interview and the alternative interview that determines whether an interviewee is offered the position. So if you feel you haven't performed well at the alternative interview, don't think that all is lost.

## Tests and group interviews

Employers may use either of these techniques in order to assess the following qualities in an individual.

### INTELLECT

Intellect can be assessed in a number of ways. The usual way to assess the intellect is to ask the interviewee questions about themselves, their experience and their ability to do the job in question. It is a lengthy method and can be misleading because interviewees can learn to give the right kind of answers. Therefore employers have learnt from their past mistakes and so they may assess the candidates' intellect by giving them a written test to do. This test might be:

- to write a short essay.
- to answer some multiple-choice questions.
- to do a piece of creative writing.
- to do some problem-solving.
- to do a numerical test.

The purpose of the written test is to assess the extent of the individual's knowledge at the time of the test. The test is normally unprepared, otherwise it is just a test of the person with the 'best memory' rather than the 'best knowledge'. Depending upon the type of test given, it can give selectors an indication of an individual's:

- knowledge of the subject.
- numerical skills.
- logical ability.
- use of grammar.

- knowledge of syntax.
- presentation skills.

An assessment can then be made of whether the person can express themselves on paper in a structured and comprehensible way.

If the test is particularly difficult, don't give up, as everyone else may be finding the test hard as well. Try to have a relaxed attitude. Do what you can, but don't worry if the test is over your head. The tests are designed to discover potential weaknesses. Remember, if you run out of time when writing an essay, it is worth doing a rough plan so selectors can see how you would have finished it, given time. Do your best, and remember that the test alone is not the deciding factor – so don't give up hope.

## PERSONALITY

Personality is key to settling into and performing in the job. As it is difficult to accurately assess an individual's personality by asking questions, some employers rely upon the results of a personality test. The true value of these tests in the selection process is a subject of some controversy, although they are widely used.

There are many different kinds of tests on the market, but on the whole these tests are designed to measure an individual's behaviour, strengths and weaknesses, and how they will behave and cope in the work environment. The types of behaviour that might be assessed on these tests are the following:

- **The level of compliance.** A compliant person is someone who likes an ordered, structured and stable work environment. He/she would be precise, conscious of detail and seldom antagonize others.

- **The level of control.** A person who likes a lot of control is wary of change, likes to do familiar tasks and to be in a group environment. A person who doesn't want control relishes change, challenge and new ideas. This person could be restless and like to steer the group.

- **Influential skills.** An influential person can persuade and influence others to his/her way of thinking. This person is usually vivacious, outgoing and friendly. On the down side, he/she can become too emotionally involved in situations and ignore the *facts* when making decisions.

- **Drive.** People who have a lot of drive tend to be dominant, competitive and direct. He/she tends to be goal-orientated and less interested in other people. Being highly ambitious, he/she may change jobs frequently to further his/her career.

- **The level of maturity.** Maturity is the ability to understand yourself and others. There is a fine line between maturity and immaturity but the test will assess the person's dependence, selfishness, self-discipline, willingness to accept responsibility, and ability to think processes through.

Some tests also indicate stress levels, both at home and at work. If a high level of stress was highlighted in your test, you would normally be questioned about this once at the interview. Thus the tests can give the employer thought-provoking insights into the person, insights which help employers to know their employees better in order to motivate them, train them and ensure that they reach their full potential.

If you are asked to do a personality test, do it, but don't make a fuss. The tests are not going to magically uncover things about you, but put into words things that you already know about yourself. Refusing to do the test could seriously damage your chances. If you want to see the results of the test, then ask, in a friendly manner, 'It would help me too if I could see the results of the test. Would that be at all possible?'

Some organizations will talk you through the results of the test afterwards, and others prefer to send you the written report by post. If neither of these options are available and you still want to know what the employers know about you, then it may be worth considering contacting a private bureau or consultancy that offers this service.

## GROOMING

You don't have to be a 'beauty', but you should look good. Grooming is vital for all interviews (see pages 29–31). For the alternative interview the employer often has all the interviewees together *en masse*. It is then easy to assess who is well or badly groomed. Remember, to be successful, you *must* be well-groomed and look professional.

## LEADERSHIP QUALITIES

Leadership is a person's ability to inspire confidence, admiration and trust in others, so that they turn to that person for guidance and help. Leadership qualities may be an important aspect of the job. Employers may want to see whether you naturally lead or are led, and also to determine your leadership style and manner. How do they do this? The usual way to do this is to have a group interview/discussion. A group discussion means that all the prospective candidates are grouped together in a room with the selectors present somewhere in the room. The selectors' role is to observe the discussion. The group may be given a subject to discuss or left in a silence for a while to see what they choose to discuss.

The purpose of the group discussion is to see how the interviewees behave under these conditions. Selectors will notice how people interact with others, how they respond, take initiative and steer and direct the conversation.

Under these circumstances it is easy for selectors to decide which people have the appropriate leadership qualities and whether their leadership is accepted by the others in the group.

**How to behave in a group situation.**

It is best to be yourself. Don't feel that you have to start the conversation off or say something just for the sake of it. It is far more important to express relevant and concise comments. In order to present a favourable impression of yourself, stick to the following points.

- **Always listen to others.** Selectors will not be impressed if you interrupt, put people down or ignore what has already been said. Wait your turn and build upon the conversation.

- **See the group as a whole rather than as a few individuals.** Avoid homing in on a particular individual, as this can have a negative effect. Try to show that you can interact with all types of people. It is worth complimenting others and referring to the other people in the group by using their first names.

- **Step in and redirect the conversation when necessary.** Don't be afraid to say that the conversation has gone off at a tangent. If *you* think it, then so do the others, but be brave and say something. Either summarize what has been mentioned so far, or suggest an idea or topic that could be discussed next.

- **Ensure that the discussion has a satisfactory ending.** Bring the conversation to an end by summarizing what has been said, taking a vote on some issue, or suggesting an ending or idea if nothing has been put forward in the discussion.

- **Talk, but don't hog the stage.** Avoid falling into the trap of doing all the talking, because it won't get you anywhere. Talk and then sit back and wait for someone to say something, even if you have to wait a while.

- **Remain calm.** The discussion may get a bit heated, but never get drawn into an argument. Express yourself in a calm manner and remain self-controlled.

- **Show motivation.** Motivation is the extent of drive within a person, enabling that individual to stick to a job, work hard at it to progress, and be a conscientious worker. Your motivation will be under scrutiny, for example your desire to earn more, to work harder, and to further your career aspirations. To discover the extent of your motivation, employers often ask about your financial background in order to find out whether you need to earn money. If you are fortunate enough not to have to earn, be cautious. To some extent employers feel 'safer' if you are dependent on them for an income. So show motivation to convince the employer that you will work hard to progress and achieve goals.

## The telephone interview

The telephone interview is common for jobs where the person will spend the majority of their time on the telephone. Selectors choose the telephone interview to screen out all the unsuitable candidates. Candidates may be unaccustomed or inexperienced at dealing with conversations over the phone. So, if your initial contact with the employer is by phone, make sure that you prepare before you dial the number. Treat the request to 'phone for more information' as the first interview.

Find out about the company, its product, its market share and its competitors. Think also about what you have to offer the company. You will need to say things like 'My areas of expertise are ...' or 'I have had experience of ...'.

The following points are worth noting:

- Speak clearly.
- Take your time and don't be frightened of periods of silence.
- Treat the recipient of the call with respect and courtesy.
- Sell yourself.
- Express interest in the job.
- End the conversation properly – don't just hang up.

## The presentation interview

Presentation interviews can either highlight a topic to prepare in advance or simply request a 30-minute presentation about the applicant. The key is to *prepare*. Having a few overhead slides can help to make a presentation more lively. The easier of the two kinds of presentation to do is the one about yourself, for you are in charge and can give a polished performance.

To give a balanced and complete performance, structure your presentation around the following points.

- **Brief educational background (10 minutes).** Give a summary of your education and training. Mention anything that was different – this might include project work or particular subjects taken. Refer to relevant work experience and talk about your relationships with people.

- **Work experience (10 minutes).** Give a brief summary of your working life to date. The key element is your achievements; by highlighting your achievements you will have greater impact. Employers will be interested in you because you add value to the company. Having completed a duty is not a plus point, it is your obligation to the company. Mention any aspirations that you have for your future. Refer also to the company that you are applying to and what knowledge you have of it so far and how you see yourself fitting in.

- **Character/interests (10 minutes).** Personality is key to an employer's choice, so try not to fall into the trap of being the 'faceless candidate'. Talk briefly about any activities that you have outside of work, as long as they don't appear too time-consuming. Show also that you can make trustworthy relationships. Refer to your strengths of character. For a presentation on a particular topic, remember to include relevant facts and figures, background information on the subject and your personal thoughts and ideas.

## The second interview

Most companies will want to meet a person again because first impressions can be deceptive. The second interview is your opportunity to meet either the Personnel Department or the next tier of management. Treat Personnel with respect, and be aware that you might also be interviewed by the person you will be replacing. By the time you reach a second interview, many more assumptions are made, namely that you understand the role.

The second interview will mostly involve discussions about:

- what you can offer the company.
- how you will resolve their problems.
- your career aspirations and plans for the future.

For greater detail, see pages 51–60. This is your chance to demonstrate that you are the most suitable candidate.

# EIGHT

## Assessing the Offer

Congratulations, you have been offered the job! All your hard work has paid off. Celebrate your success and *then* take time to consider the offer objectively. Do you accept the offer or do you reject it? Just because you have been offered a job doesn't mean that you automatically have to accept it. The job *has* to be the right career move for you.

This chapter demonstrates what you need to assess in order to make your final decision. It also shows you how to negotiate an arrangement that satisfies both you and the employer if the need arises. If it is a job that you really want, don't keep the employer hanging on for your reply, but accept it quickly. If, on the other hand, the offer isn't quite right, don't be in too much of a hurry to reject it. Talk to the prospective employer and try to settle mutually agreeable terms. Thus, it is necessary to weigh up the offer and to be convinced that this is the next step for you.

A job offer must be in writing. Only then can it be regarded as worthy and solid. If it isn't in writing, specifying terms and conditions, pay and start date then *it is not an offer*. Don't rely upon someone's word; they can forget what they've said or simply change their mind. So a verbal 'We're interested in you' isn't good enough. If in doubt, get the employer to make his offer in writing. Then, one way or another, the employer will be forced to make up his mind about you. Only hand in your notice with your current employer when you have received a written offer from the new employer. Never do it beforehand, as the offer you are waiting for may never arrive and you could then be confronted with having to crawl back to your current employer, or with looking for yet another job. Be safe and beware of the verbal offer.

## Points to consider

Only you can decide whether you really want the job on offer, but the points listed below are worth considering.

### HOW BADLY DO YOU NEED THIS JOB?

Money normally plays a part here and affects the ultimate decision. For example, if your financial situation needs improving because of debts or unemployment, or your finances are causing you stress, then see the job as an opportunity to put yourself on an even footing again. The key is to be realistic about the urgency of the situation and take action accordingly.

If, on the other hand, you are in work and your current salary is satisfactory, don't just accept the job because it has been offered. When in work you can afford to be selective and wait for the right job to crop up. However, before you reject this offer consider how you will feel in a year's time if you are still in the same job and still looking for another job. Would you be happy with the decision you had made, or would you regret your decision? Regret is destructive and negative, so try to avoid it at all costs. It might only be a matter of time before the job you are after crops up. Then you would be pleased you had waited.

### DOES THIS JOB FIT INTO YOUR LONG-TERM CAREER PATH?

Successful people plan their careers. They have a clearly thought-out idea of what they want to do in the present and also over the next five, ten and maybe fifteen years. They take jobs not just because of the money, increased responsibility or the profile but also because it fits into their career plan. If you don't have a plan of some kind it is easy to get sidetracked or distracted, or to take jobs that don't give long-term satisfaction. For example, people often choose to go abroad in order to earn 'big bucks'. Earning money is important, but it is far more crucial to have a long-term plan.

So an overseas job that pays 'loads of money' needs to offer *valuable* and *relevant* experience, experience that is recognized and transferable to your country of origin or the environment where you want to work afterwards. Otherwise, although money lures you, it could commit and trap you into working abroad for the rest of your career, as returning to your home country could mean a huge backward step, a step you may not be prepared to take.

## WEIGHING UP THE OFFER

It is necessary to weigh up the job and consider all that it offers, both good and bad. Unfortunately, most people don't do this. Instead they only assess the *benefits* of the new job, the feel-good factor from being offered 'this superb job', and also the enormous boost their ego will get. So the decision is made by bundling all the benefits of the new job together and comparing them with the negatives of the present job.

For example, the benefits could be:

- a job with a bigger, more prestigious company and products.
- the opportunity of foreign travel.
- reporting directly to the Director.

These are compared with the negative aspects of the current job: being office-bound, not being able to get on with the boss, and the low image of the current role. The person may forget however, what he/she may be giving up:

- private medical care.
- company car/pension.
- two years' service.
- comfort and security of current role.

- track record.

- company's internal promotion policy.

So the message is to assess the new job in a balanced way, not in an emotional way. For it may be that the benefits are not all that good, anyway – foreign travel may not be as often as the person would like, and the Director may be difficult to get on with. Always ensure that you gain more than you lose. See the new job for what it really is, rather than through rose-coloured glasses. To do this, imagine yourself doing the new job day in, day out, every day for a year; will it still give you the same buzz after a year of actually doing it? What are the pressures that you will have to face? What are the exciting bits? If you think you will enjoy the job after you have considered everything, especially the less glamorous parts then you have done everything you could possibly do to assess the suitability of the post. Then, if it turns out to be better than you expected, you know you made the right decision. If, on the other hand, it doesn't turn out quite right and you have a few nasty surprises, then at least you know that you did everything you could possibly have done in reaching your decision.

So, in order to gain a fair and realistic view, balance the gains against the losses. Does this change your decision?

## DO YOU FIT IN WITH THE COMPANY?

How did you feel at the interview? Is this the right place for you to work? Would you fit in as you are, or do you need to change certain things about yourself in order to be accepted? It is vital that the chemistry between you and the company is right.

## CHECK THE COMPANY OUT ONE LAST TIME

Your job offer is normally made subject to satisfactory references and medical report. Thus the company will check you out fully and will rarely take any risks. You need to adopt the same tactics. If you got away with not doing some research before the interview, now is the time to do it. Ring up the Company Secretary's department, or the Marketing department, and ask for the annual report and brochures to be sent to you. Then check the following details.

- How long the company has been in existence.

- The Chairman's or Chief Executive's comments. These statements will give you an idea of the philosophy of the company and an inclination of future growth, expansion and projects.

- What the company does or makes (a client of mine at a Consulting Engineering firm had, in the past, graduates applying who didn't even know what a Consulting Engineer was).

- The financial position of the company – turnover, profit, training costs etc. If these are not listed in the brochure, refer to the *Financial Times*.

It may be in your interest to arrange a visit to have a detailed look around the company and to meet your future colleagues. Then you might pick up on the culture, philosophy and attitude of the business. If you have the time, it is worth doing, as it is a good way to reconfirm that this is the right move for you.

## *Improving the offer through negotiation*

Normally the offer letter contains no surprises in terms of pay and conditions. Usually these are discussed at the interview, and, although the exact salary figure may not have been quoted, the offer is within the range. It is not until the company chooses the preferred candidate that the salary figure is discussed in terms of pounds and pence. As a general rule, salary is determined by:

- what the company is accustomed to paying.
- what your current salary is.
- your level of experience and expertise.

In terms of a salary increase, it is usually 10–20 per cent higher than your current salary. It would probably not be as high as this, however, if you are changing profession or have been out of the workforce for a long period of time.

If the offer letter doesn't satisfy your desires and needs, you can either accept it, say nothing and enter your new job perhaps with feelings of resentment, or you can take action. Shed any embarrassment and stand up for what you want and feel you have been promised. You now enter into a negotiation phase with the employer. There is no doubt that negotiation is not easy but if you deal with it in a professional way you could achieve a better offer.

The basic principles are the same whatever you are negotiating. Successful negotiation is about achieving a win-win situation not a win-lose one, i.e. a conclusion that satisfies both parties, not where one party is forced into submission or withdrawal. So consider your own needs, but also take into account the employer's needs and constraints. If you adopt and adapt the following principles you will increase your chances of success.

## DECIDE WHO HOLDS THE POWER

Who holds the power – you or the employer? Don't leap to conclusions, because the answer may not be what you expect it to be. How much power you have determines how high your demands can be.

You hold the power if:

- the interview went exceptionally well.
- you are convinced you are the best candidate (perhaps you have been told).
- the offer came in very quickly.

- you are a specialist in your field.
- the company have a particular problem that urgently needs resolving and you both know that you are the person to sort out the problem.
- you hold competitive information.
- you have knowledge the employer wants.
- the employer approached you, not the other way round

The employer holds the power if:

- you are just the best of the bunch
- the employer was nonchalant at the interview
- the employer was distant
- the employer was vague at the interview and wouldn't disclose certain things about the job or company
- the offer took a long time to come in
- you know there is another strong internal candidate – it is then a two-horse race
- the position is newly created – they don't have to fill it
- the employer has held a number of interviews

The balance of power will determine how high or low you pitch your opening bid.

## DECIDE WHAT YOU WANT

You can't enter negotiations unless you know what you want. Decide what it is you are after and also know what you would be prepared to accept if your demands aren't fully met. So know what you want, but also what your walk-away position is. A walk-away position is the point at which the negotiation breaks down; this will be different for each individual, according to personal circumstances. For example, one person might not accept a job unless the conditions are changed; another might give negotiation a try and even if their demands aren't met they will accept the job. For example, if a person is threatened with redundancy or unemployment, the walk-away position may be different from that of someone who is already employed.

Negotiation is normally over salary. For example, a client of mine was verbally offered a salary in the interview of between £30,000 and £33,000. However, the offer letter quoted a salary figure of £29,500 – the same as his current salary. He was disappointed that there was no increase in money, especially as it had been hinted at in the interview. The client decided he wanted an increase of some sort, and his walk-away position was that unless he achieved this he wouldn't take the job.

## PUTTING YOUR CASE FORWARD

It is advisable to test the water verbally first, and then if need be put your case in writing. Ring up the person who made the offer, but if this person didn't interview you speak to the interviewer. The first rule is to be firm and friendly but not aggressive. Aggressive behaviour is matched by an aggressive response and then negotiations tend to break down altogether. So the key is to stay calm at all costs. Adopt a businesslike manner and choose your wording carefully. Avoid allocating blame, criticizing the person, or 'huffing and puffing'. Try to avoid comments like 'Well, you know I was looking for a salary figure of £33,000, so this figure of £29,500 is nowhere near acceptable'. It is much better to say something along the lines of 'Thank you for the offer. I am ready and keen to accept it as soon as the salary is finalized. I was disappointed to see that the salary you are quoting is £29,500.' Then you need to state what you want, dependent upon the balance of power. If you hold the power, suggest a reasonably high figure, such as 'I would be prepared to accept £32,500'.

This opens up the discussion. The employer will give you his/her opinion. He/she will either accept your figure or reject it. If it is rejected, negotiation goes further. If it is a blunt 'No, I can't accept that', ask the employer what he/she would offer. If he/she won't budge on the original figure, show that you understand the reasons for this – perhaps there is a fixed salary budget, or other internal salary levels to consider. Offer instead some tradeables (things that you would accept instead), for example:

- a salary review after a specified period of time.
- overtime pay.
- a shortening of the period of time after which you will be able to buy company shares.
- benefits of a higher grade, such as pension entitlements, medical or company car rights.
- a greater holiday entitlement.

Share your ideas and offer your tradeables. The employer will either agree or disagree, and you can then both reach a satisfactory conclusion to the discussions. Once terms have been agreed, ask the employer to issue you with another offer letter including the agreed new terms.

## Handing in your notice

This is not an easy thing to do, whether you like or dislike your present company. The company could also make your decision harder by offering you an enhanced package to stay with them. However, the best thing you can do in this situation is leave, because sweeteners won't satisfy you in the long term. If you have decided to leave and think you have found a better job, stick by your decision. The chances are if you do decide to stay, you will probably be looking for another job again before long. Remember that the dissatisfactions you have with your current company won't go away.

However, talk things through with your boss, and above all, stay on good terms. Don't be tempted to use your notice period as an opportunity to get back at people! Remain professional throughout and keep your negative thoughts and opinions on how things could run better to yourself. Continue to perform in your job, as you are after a decent reference. Remember never to fall out with anyone, as you never know when you might need your old company, colleagues or bosses again.

## What to do if the new job is not suitable

This may seem unthinkable, but it does happen (although not often). You start the job and within a short period of time you realize you have made an awful mistake. In fact you would do anything to have your old job back. You could look for another job, but this is risky because of your lack of service in your current job. The best option you have is to contact your previous employer. This is not a sign of defeat but a sensible move. Anyway, perhaps the company haven't appointed your replacement yet, or maybe your replacement isn't that impressive. Ring up your old boss and arrange a meeting. If you do go back, though, try to sort out beforehand any differences that you had. In fact, the separation period may have done you both the world of good.

# NINE

# Conclusion

Interviews are stressful occasions. You can however ease the burden by being prepared and by adopting the right attitude. Try to adopt the philosophy that 'you win some, you lose some'. Try not to take things too seriously and avoid thinking that some situations are more hopeful than others, because, if things don't work out as you would like, you will have to work hard to pick yourself up again. Try to have a conversation with the interviewer, rather than just answering the questions posed.

Remember that the objective of an interview is not to talk to the interviewer about yourself but to communicate your ability, willingness and suitability for the job. Don't be afraid to reveal details about yourself, as it will work to your advantage. Take the stage and shine.

## What to do if you are not offered the job

Being rejected is tough, but rejection affects everyone differently. Some people bounce back quickly because they don't let frustration build up inside them. They do something positive and improve their performance or they get rid of their frustration physically – by doing sport, gardening or a favourable leisure activity. However, some people take rejection more personally, and so it can be a tough time. Given time, effort and practice, it is possible to improve that performance of yours.

## TRY NOT TO TAKE REJECTION PERSONALLY

Try, in what ever way you can, to get rid of the emotion. Being emotionally upset and disappointed is time-wasting. You could be putting all that effort into applying for an equally suitable position. Keep active and apply for something else. Don't despair, because you may have been truly brilliant and just missed the job by a whisker. Anyway, you will receive far more rejection slips than acceptances, because it is a fact of life that far more candidates are rejected from job applications than accepted.

## LEARN SOMETHING FROM THE EXPERIENCE

What can you learn from your experience? How did you feel after the interview? Did you do enough pre-interview preparation? Looking back now, was it your best possible performance? Rarely is everything bad, but there may be a number of areas that need to be perfected. Read the following words and phrases and circle any that you think may be lacking from your performance.

| | |
|---|---|
| Ambition | Knowledge |
| Awareness of company/job | Leadership qualities |
| Communication | Motivation |
| Compatibility | Openness |
| Conciseness | Personality |
| Confidence | Pleasant appearance |
| Drive | Positive attitude |
| Efficiency | Preparation |
| Enthusiasm | Professionalism |
| Flexibility | Qualifications |
| Formality | Related work experience |
| Grooming | Self-control |
| Intellect | |

In addition, you may want to ring up the interviewer to gather information on how to improve your application or interview performance. (The forms shown in the Appendix will give you an idea of how an employer will assess your application and interview.) Avoid challenging the person's decision, because he/she will only clam up and defend the decision or withhold vital information. Some people are reluctant to give the 'exact reason' for rejection; some may not even remember who you are; but some will be helpful. They might put your mind at rest by telling you that you were a close second or that the job wasn't filled due to internal circumstances. So, from the highlighted words and the interviewer's feedback, you will have something to work on. Either get a friend or partner to help you, or consider paying for a professional company to help you resolve some of the issues raised.

*Good luck!*

# Appendix – Useful Forms

---

**CONFIDENTIAL**

**INTERVIEW REPORT AND ASSESSMENT FORM**

**1  CANDIDATE DETAILS**

   Name of candidate: _____

   Current contact address: _____

   _____

   _____

   PHOTO

   Postcode: _____ Telephone: _____ .

   Source: ☐ Advert ☐ CRS ☐ Spec ☐ Other

**2  INTERVIEW DETAILS**

   Interview date: _____ Time: _____

   To see: _____ (Personnel)

   _____ (Department)

**3  ACADEMIC/PROFESSIONAL ACHIEVEMENTS**

   Secondary: _____

   Undergraduate/postgraduate: _____

   Other: _____

   Languages: _____

   Plans for further studies: _____

   Membership of Institutions: _____

   Published Work: _____

| 4 | **WORK HISTORY AND OTHER COMMENTS** |

_____
_____
_____
_____
_____
_____
_____
_____
_____
_____

Reasons for leaving past/present job:
_____

References:
_____

| 5 | **MOTIVATION/ASPIRATIONS** |

Long-term aspirations:
_____

Particular aspects of work in which interested:
_____

Other applications: _____
Interviews? _____
Offers? _____

| 6 | **FLEXIBILITY/MOBILITY** |

Places willing to work? _____
Overseas/for how long? _____
Driving licence? _____ Own car? _____
Other: _____

| | |
|---|---|
| 7 | **PERSONAL/INTERESTS** |

Health? _____ Smoker? _____

Hospital/days off in last year? _____

Disability/illness? _____

Interests: _____

Sports/social: _____

| | |
|---|---|
| 8 | **REMUNERATION PACKAGE** |

Current salary/benefits: _____
(Holiday/Pension/PPP/bonus etc)

Salary expectations? _____

Notice period/available? _____

| | |
|---|---|
| 9 | **INTERVIEW ASSESSMENT** |

Personnel interviewer _____

Signed: _____ Date: _____

Departmental interviewer

Signed: _____ Date: _____

| | |
|---|---|
| 10 | **RECOMMENDATION** |

Make offer: ☐ Position: _____ Requisition No: _____

Grade: _____ Salary: _____

Do not make offer: ☐ Give reasons: _____

_____

_____

_____

_____

**CONFIDENTIAL**

**GRADUATE INTERVIEW REPORT AND ASSESSMENT FORM**

Name of candidate: _____ Interview date: _____

_____ To see: _____

Age: _____ Time: _____

Why this career? _____

_____

_____

_____

**Particular aspects of work in which interested:** _____

_____

**Technical strengths:** _____

_____

**Technical weaknesses:** _____

_____

**Has the candidate sufficient knowledge for this position?** _____

_____

**Further education:** _____

_____

**Secondary education:** _____

_____

**Plans for further study:** _____

_____

**Languages (levels 1, 2, 3, 4)** _____

_____

1 = O Level

2 = A Level

3 = Degree

4 = Bilingual/Native

Computer skills/
experience:

Work and holiday
experience:

Other activities:

Places willing to
work:

Salary sought:

Driving licence:

Own car?

Health:

Smoker: Yes/No

Other interviews/
offers received:

When available:

References:

## SUMMARY

|  | Maximum | Actual |
|---|---|---|
| Impact – what impression? | 10 | |
| Qualifications and experience | 10 | |
| Communication skills | 10 | |
| Motivation – how strong? | 10 | |
| Environment – how will the candidate fit in? | 10 | |
| TOTAL | 50 | |

Other comments: _____

Interviewer's signature: _____

Definite offer: ☐   Further consideration: ☐   Not suitable: ☐

# Index

academic questions 53
acceptance letters 47
aggressive behaviour 95
alternative interviews 79–87
　group discussion 83–5
　presentations 86
　telephone 85
　tests 80–2
angry attitudes 38–9
answering questions 69–70, 72
appearance 29–31, 46, 74
application forms 25
arguments 13
arriving for interviews 10–11, 46, 71
asking questions 61–8
　active approach 65–6
　and attitude 64–5
　company-orientated 66–7
　on job input 63
　passive approach 65–6
　repetitive questions 62
　revealing drive/ambition 63–4
　self-orientated 66–7
　time available 68
　*see also* questions
attitude 35–44
　importance 37
　mental attitude 26–7
　negative 38–42
　positive 26–7, 42–4
　when asking questions 64–5

behaviour assessments 81–2
being yourself 69
body language 28–9, 70

career plans 22, 57, 87, 89–90
chances of success 10
children 49
clarification questions 52–3
closed questions 16
closing interviews 76–8
clothes 29–31, 46, 74
company philosophies 12–13, 91
company research 91
company-orientated questions 57–9, 66–7
competitiveness 45
complicated questions 18
compliments 33
confidence 7–9
　inspiring 8–9
　qualities 7–8
criticizing interviewers 75

# Index

crossing legs  28
current employment  55–6
   notice periods  88, 96–7
CVs (curriculum vitae)  25, 37

depressive attitudes  38
desperate attitudes  39
dress  29–31, 46, 74

easy questions  48
embarrassing interviewers  74
emotionally unstable
   attitudes  40
employers' concerns  9
energy levels  45
enthusiasm  49, 70, 72
environment  26
evening interviews  72, 74

factual questions  52–3
family questions  48–52
farewells  78
feedback  9
format of interviews  12

grooming  29–31, 46, 83
group discussion  83–5

hairstyle  29–30
half-hearted attitudes  39–40
historical questions  53–6
hobbies  51
hours of work  50–1
hypothetical questions  17, 59–60

image  29–31
intellect assessments  80–1
interview rooms  26
interviewers  13–14
   criticizing  75
   embarrassing  74
   rapport with  31–3, 71

introductions  32
irrational attitudes  41

job input  63
job suitability  22, 73, 97
job-related questions  53–6
jokes  74

know-it-all attitudes  40

leadership qualities  45, 83–5
leading questions  17–18
learning from the experience  99–100
listening  62, 71, 84
loyalty  54, 70
lunchtime interviews  72, 74

manners  71, 74
marital status  49
medical reports  91
mental attitude  26–7
motivation  29, 49, 84–5
moving-on techniques  14

name-dropping  74
negative attitudes  38–42
negotiation  92–6
nerves  8, 11, 23–8
   calming  23–4
   common fears  23
   focusing on others  25, 32
non-conformist attitudes  41–2
non-verbal signals  28
notice periods  88, 96–7

open questions  14–16
opinions  13
opportunist attitudes  38
overseas jobs  90

panels  11
personal questions  48–52

personality   69
personality tests   81–2
personnel departments   87
planning ability   45
positive attitudes   26–7, 42–4
power   93–4
practice   12, 27–8
presentations   86
pressure   50
previous employment   53–4, 56, 70
probing questions   16–17
purpose of interviews   9–10

questions   12–19, 47–60
  academic   53
  answering   69–70, 72
  clarification   52–3
  closed   16
  company related   57–9
  complicated   18
  easy   48
  factual   52–3
  hypothetical   17, 59–60
  job-related   53–6
  leading   17–18
  open   14–16
  personal/family   48–52
  preparing for   47
  probing   16–17
  reflecting on   19
  summarizing   18–19
  visionary   56–7
  *see also* asking questions

rapport   31–3, 71
realistic attitudes   44
references   91

rehearsal   12, 27–8
rejection   98–9
repetitive questions   62

salaries   55, 57, 89
  negotiating   92–3, 95–6
seating arrangements   11
second interviews   87
self-appraisal   44–5
self-confidence   7–9
self-discipline   45
self-orientated questions   66–7
setting the scene   13–14
skills   51
sloppy attitudes   41, 45
smoking   73–4
strengths   51–2
stress levels   82
structure of interviews   11–12
summarizing questions   18–19

telephone interviews   85
tests   80–2
time to ask questions   68
travelling to interviews   46
  *see also* arriving for interviews

unemployed periods   54

verbal job offers   88
videos   27
visionary attitudes   42
visionary questions   56–7

weaknesses   52
weighing up offers   90–1
written job offers   88
written tests   80–2